Philade[lphia]
on the Fly

ron P. swegman

Illustrations by the author

Dedication

For my family,
For my friends

Acknowledgements

Special thanks to Alan L. Gordon and Oliver C. Shell, who read the manuscript and provided invaluable angling advice, and Michael L. Kaufmann, Area Fisheries Manager – SE, Pennsylvania Fish & Boat Commission, who generously offered his expertise. Thanks also to Ketan Ben Caesar, Steve "Fishing Without A Net" Detofsky, Jim Gladstone, Leonard Gontarek, Samantha Kafky, Dwight Landis, Ted Leeson, Kimberly Maxwell, John Mutone, Brynne Orlando, Leonard Reuter, Joe E. Shaughnessy, Greg Smith, Lamont B. Steptoe, Fred Trassati, Chamyang "wojo" Unkow, Emily Violet, and all the fine fisher folk who offered stories or smiles along the water.

"A River Revival" first appeared in *River Smallies*; "Catfish Friday" first appeared in *La Petite Zine*; an excerpt from "Hippie Trout" first appeared in *Pennsylvania Fly Fishing*; "Why Lines?" and an excerpt from "Fishing Without A Net" were performed live on WXPN 88.5 FM Philadelphia as part of the "Live At The Writers House" radio program sponsored by the University of Pennsylvania.

© 2005 ron P. swegman

Frank Amato Publications, Inc, P.O. Box 82112, Portland, Oregon 97282

503.653.8108 • www.amatobooks.com

All photographs by the author unless otherwise noted.
Chapter Illustrations by ron P. swegman
Book & Cover Design: Kathy Johnson
Map Illustrations by Kathy Johnson
Printed in Singapore

Softbound ISBN: 1-57188-361-4   UPC: 0-81127-00195-8

1 3 5 7 9 10 8 6 4 2

Contents

Wissahickon Creek & The Wissahickon Valley

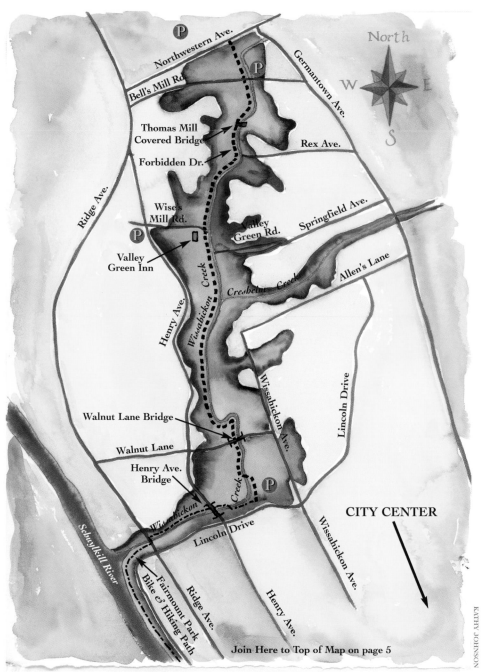

North

W · E

S

Northwestern Ave.

Bell's Mill Rd.

Germantown Ave.

Thomas Mill
Covered Bridge

Rex Ave.

Forbidden Dr.

Wise's
Mill Rd.

Valley
Green Rd.

Springfield Ave.

Valley
Green Inn

Cresheim Creek

Allen's Lane

Henry Ave.

Wissahickon Creek

Wissahickon Ave.

Lincoln Drive

Walnut Lane Bridge

Walnut Lane

Henry Ave.
Bridge

Creek

CITY CENTER

Schuylkill River

Wissahickon

Lincoln Drive

Wissahickon Ave.

Fairmount Park
Bike & Hiking Path

Ridge Ave.

Henry Ave.

Join Here to Top of Map on page 5

KATHY JOHNSON

Fairmount Park Bike and Hiking Path ▬·▬·▬·▬
Forbidden Drive ▬ ▬ ▬ ▬ ▬
Parking Ⓟ

Schuylkill River & Fairmount Park

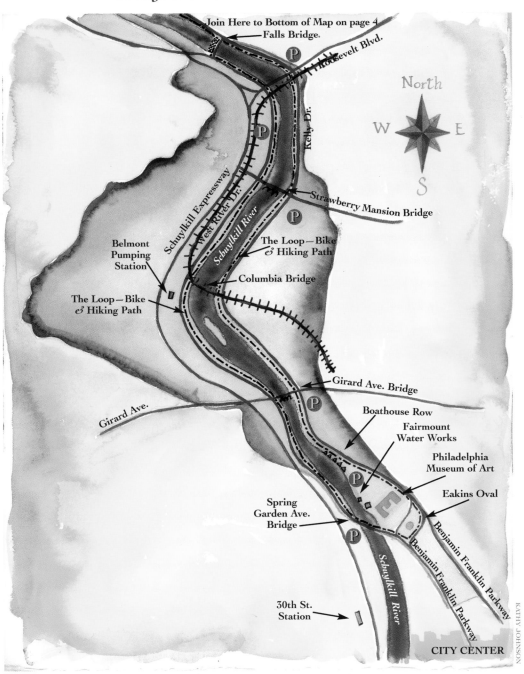

Join Here to Bottom of Map on page 4
Falls Bridge.

Roosevelt Blvd.

North

W E

S

Kelly Dr.

Strawberry Mansion Bridge

Schuylkill Expressway

West River Dr.

Schuylkill River

Belmont Pumping Station

The Loop—Bike & Hiking Path

Columbia Bridge

The Loop—Bike & Hiking Path

Girard Ave. Bridge

Girard Ave.

Boathouse Row

Fairmount Water Works

Philadelphia Museum of Art

Eakins Oval

Spring Garden Ave. Bridge

Benjamin Franklin Parkway

Benjamin Franklin Parkway

Schuylkill River

30th St. Station

CITY CENTER

KATHY JOHNSON

The Loop—Bike & Hiking Path ▬ ▪ ▬ ▪ ▬
Train Tracks ┼┼┼┼┼┼┼┼┼┼
Parking Ⓟ

Map 5

Prologue

Muddler Minnow

Why Lines?

Why do I fish? Why do I write? The answer, it seems, is a specific type of solitude. Both activities embody this state of being. I never have been one to shy away from people, but there always has been a desire to experience the new alone, to test the limits of my own abilities, to document what I have seen and provide the first person, eyewitness account. There is the satisfaction of self-sufficiency, the poetics of the process, and at the end of the lines, if one is lucky, there remains something special and lasting—

A story . . .

Walnut Lane Bridge, b. 1907: once the world's largest
poured-concrete structure, Wissahickon Creek.

Chapter 1

Elk Hair Caddis

Earth Day

I pushed myself a littler harder, pedaled a little farther, and the reward was my discovery of Wissahickon Creek.

My drive had been the desire to scout this stream on my mountain bike. The Wissahickon was included on Pennsylvania's list of approved trout streams, and most of the creek fell within Philadelphia's city limits. I read these facts in the magazine published by the Pennsylvania Fish & Boat Commission, and I was both excited and astonished. Here was an urban trout stream, one I could cycle to from my front door! The page had handed me a present.

I had often felt the urge to fly-fish: that tingling, physical sensation of excitement all anglers have experienced, especially near the opening day of trout season, but I had never acted on it. The pastel days of early spring always passed too quickly for the spark to catch fire, and other passions would lead me into another summer in the city. Ten years went by in this way—

A decade away from the water.

I had moved to the city directly from college, and my career, my creative writing, and my circle of companions kept me busy within Center City. Yet something was missing, and something had changed.

Perhaps I had simply woven myself too tightly into the urban fabric. Routine had become rut. The cafés and taverns had become claustrophobic; I could rarely sit and read without being interrupted. The streets and the buildings had become too familiar; my passion for the city's great architecture had cooled. I needed contrast, the wilderness, to balance my moribund cosmopolitan perspective.

Running and biking had become my main outdoor recreations, but neither ever involved me within nature. I was at best a swiftly passing observer of the landscape. The water and the trees and the birds flew by like a film whenever I cycled "The Loop" that follows the Schuylkill River from the Philadelphia Museum of Art up to the Falls Bridge and back. The connection was visual, not three-dimensional. What I wanted was an experience where the outdoors suffused inside my body and mind. This is fly-fishing.

When I began to have winter dreams about cycling from the city to a stream where I caught trout and bass, I knew I must find a place to fly-fish, if only to satisfy my restless psyche's demand for some intimacy with woods and water. These angling dreams were an expression of a desire, barely buried, to return to that aspect of my youth that had been instrumental in shaping the person I had become. This desire was rising to the surface, and it expressed itself as the need to explore the natural world. And there was the sentimental wish, too, to have a reunion with the reliable boyhood companion I knew then, as now, as a Pennsylvania freestone stream.

I found myself with these feelings at a girlfriend's birthday party at the end of March. She introduced me to one of her fellow graduate students who I soon learned fished for trout in the Catskills. Another fisherman overheard our conversation and joined us with his own fish story. He spent his summer vacations along Cape Cod, fly-fishing from a kayak for striped bass and bluefish. My ambition was much more modest—to cast small flies along a small Pennsylvania stream—still, their tales, added to my memories, equaled the critical mass that motivated me into action.

So, here I was, greeting Wissahickon Creek for the first time. Trout season had opened a week before this April day, but no clock was counting me tardy as I reached the end of the Fairmount Park Bike and Hiking Path. A bronze plaque affixed to a fieldstone marker at this spot read:

THE FAIRMOUNT PARK BIKE AND HIKING PATH
FROM FORBIDDEN DRIVE
IN THE WISSAHICKON VALLEY
TO THE ART MUSEUM IN CENTER CITY
WAS COMPLETED BY THE CITY OF PHILADELPHIA
FAIRMOUNT PARK COMMISSION IN 1980

I looked out onto a sharp bend in the swift, rocky stream. Huge boulders had created narrow runs and pocket water at the tail end of a long pool marking the end of the Wissahickon Valley. The trail known as Forbidden Drive begins here. (This is a gray gravel path for hikers, cyclists, and horseback riders that follows the Wissahickon upstream for several miles until it reaches the campus of Chestnut Hill College.)

The creek looked as wild and as picturesque as any remote mountain stream. No development was visible except for the entrance to the Drive. It would be a stretch to say this area has remained as pristine as the land the native Lenni Lenape people knew, but the Fairmount Park Commission's preservation efforts were obvious that morning.

Then it occurred to me—it was Earth Day—a crisp, clear, perfect Sunday morning. This coincidence spoke to me. More than a validation, it was the punctuation mark to a dream achieved.

I pushed off to scout for fishing spots. Now that I knew how easy it was to get to the stream, and how fine the stream was, the challenge could be redirected to focus on the most exciting one of all: how to fish for these Philadelphia trout on the fly.

The stream below offered so many possibilities that I instantly scheduled trips for the next several weekends. I was going to give myself a lot of casting practice, and my friends were going to find a "Gone Fishing" sign hanging from my front doorknob.

Opportunity wasn't knocking—it was on the other side of an already open door—and the view it offered was the first extended stretch of postcard perfect trout water. A series of three plunge pools lined by wide, majestic boulders tumbled below a rusticated bluestone bridge built in 1897. The pools were jade green in color and separated by short stretches of riffles.

I paused and contemplated the beauty before me. I leaned my bike against the wood rail fence that lined the Drive and looked down through the trees to the dry cobbled bank that bordered my side of the

Trail Marker along Forbidden Drive, Wissahickon Creek.

stream. I spied a man my age, 30ish, dressed in khaki and olive fly-fishing apparel. He was walking downstream toward me. As he came close I saw the fly rod in his right hand, the green fly line, the wooden catch-and-release net hanging from his fishing vest. All of the old feelings I had come to know as a teenage angler returned to me within a single rush of adrenaline-charged excitement. He obviously shared this feeling, too. He had a huge smile his face could barely contain.

"Excuse me," I said. "I'm a fly-fisher. Have you had any luck here?"

"Hi! I sure have!" He pointed upstream. "In that pool. I just caught a 12-inch rainbow trout on a size 12 Elk Hair Caddis."

"You're kidding! A rainbow on a dry fly this early in the season!"

"I know!" he beamed. "Trout fishing just a fifteen-minute drive from the skyscrapers downtown!"

"Good luck!" I said. I had many more questions ready, but I didn't want to dilute the happiness of his moment. Besides, I could learn plenty by watching him cast for a few minutes. He made a good model. I admired the stealth of his streamside manner, the ease of his overhead casts, the soft roll out of the fly line that landed his Elk Hair Caddis on the surface of the pool.

So this was Wissahickon Creek. I now had a face to match the name. The clarity and swiftness of the flowing water . . . the bright, big stones . . . the new green beginning to revitalize the trees and cover the forest floor . . . I had found what I was looking for— fly-fishing, and more.

I continued upstream. The sound of my bike tires rolling along on the gravel trail was hypnotic. I progressed slowly and arched back my neck so I could contemplate the canopy of trees slowly passing by overhead. Streams of pale sunlight fingered hazy rays through the branches. Several species of birds sang simultaneously, filling the air with contrasting melodies that somehow avoided cacophony.

I passed beneath the massive center arch of the Walnut Lane Bridge, once the world's largest poured concrete structure, and made another mile of progress before reaching a long stretch of rapids. There, at the bottom of the gorge, I spied another solitary fly-fisher. I stopped and watched him work the water. He was wading, midstream, making upstream casts along the undercut bank. His chartreuse fly line drifted with the current, passed him, and at this point he shifted his rod tip to the right to make a mend that corrected the bellying of his line so the fly could continue toward some surface rocks near the end of the pool. After its float, he made another cast. A-One-And-A-Two whip of the long pole placed his fly against a long, flat boulder twenty feet above him. The line drifted down again, but this time, near the tail end, he raised his rod, which acquired a familiar deep bend.

He played the trout well, leading it to his side where he unhooked the fly as the fish lay sideways on the surface of the stream; a fine display of the catch-and-release technique that is so much a part of the fly-fishing tradition.

I sensed he could feel my presence at this point, so I pushed forward to a fork in the trail. I took the right path that led downhill to a little bridge that crossed a bend in the stream; I paused on the span and caught sight of two more fly-fishers working a stretch together.

The trail on the opposite side of the bridge narrowed quickly and became much more challenging. Furrows, loose soil, and rocks tested my mountain biking skills. I at last dismounted at the bottom of a steep dip and walked my bike the rest of the way to the pool where the two men were fishing. There, just off the trail, I came upon another fieldstone marker surrounded by bright yellow buttercups and wild purple violets. I crouched down to examine the bronze plaque, which read:

THE FIRST BAPTISMAL SERVICE
OF THE
CHURCH OF THE BRETHREN
IN AMERICA
TOOK PLACE ON THIS SITE
ON CHRISTMAS DAY
1723

So this was a sacred place with a history: another coincidence on this Earth Day Sunday. I looked up at the two fishermen in the background. Their blue fly lines floated gracefully from the air, to the stream, and back into the air. The casts were directed toward an immense boulder that shaped the bend along the opposite bank. I could easily picture men and women receiving a sacrament in this pool. The smooth flowing water and the huge, clean stone suggested the clarity, purity, and eternity of the spirit.

I walked down to the bank behind the fishermen, taking care to keep my bike from making any sudden noise. They stood side by side in knee-deep water and were casting dry flies. One looked to be about forty, the other seventy; a father and a son who had probably fly-fished together for decades, judging from the fluid counterpoint of their casts.

"Do you mind if I watch for a while?"

"Not at all," said the son.

"They keep looking at it," said the father. "They're rising, but not quite taking it."

The son nodded. When he paused to change his fly pattern I took the opportunity to ask another question:

"Is your rod a 5-weight?" I wanted to let them know their audience was one of them.

"It's a three, actually," the son said. "It has a nice, easy action for these fish."

I watched them work the pool until I finished my bottle of spring water. I recounted the past few hours: I had discovered the stream; found three good spots; felt the fraternity of fly-fishing. This was an excellent start. I quietly left them, dipped behind the bushes along the bank, and walked back up to the marker. I touched it for luck, mounted my bike, and began to pedal back toward Center City, my mind already contemplating my return with rod and reel.

Chapter 2

Light Cahill

First Day on the Fly

My new fly rod arrived the following week via express mail. I didn't want to risk any chance of losing it on its journey, the library where I worked was lenient about sending and receiving mail, and after some thought I decided it was best to have it sent to my office. I found the tall, narrow package resting against my workstation when I returned from my lunch hour. A yellow post-it note attached to the top of it read:

> What is this?
> —A

I replied with an email:

SUBJECT: The Mystery Package
A:
Thank you!
To answer your question . . . The contents contained within are a certified deadly weapon—if you are a trout. It's my new fly rod.

> Regards,
> —me

I perceived more than a few strange looks on my stroll home from work that day. Some may have thought I was carrying a rifle through the streets of Philadelphia, judging from some of the suspicious stares I received!

I did not open the package the minute I got home. I showered, changed into comfortable clothes, opened a bottle, and poured myself a glass of hearty red. I was teasing myself, adding a pleasant tension to the moment. When the time came to open the container, I did so slowly, carefully, first pulling each individual staple out of the sutured top end of the package. I pulled out the long cardboard tube within, popped the cap, and removed the long green rod case, which both protected the rod and made it convenient for travel. I twisted off the black rubber cap at one end and withdrew a long, green cloth bag. I pulled open the Velcro flap, withdrew the two sections one at a time, and jointed it together. I had it at last —

Eight and one half feet of fishing machine.

Next came the reel. I was surprised to find the manufacturer had made it easy for me by adding the Dacron backing and fly line before it was shipped. It already had its full, comfortable, ready-to-fish weight. This relieved me from an hour of knots and potential headaches. I locked the reel into place at the base of the cork handle and balanced the entire outfit on my outstretched left index finger —

Perfect!

During the following evenings I devised a system to carry my rod on my mountain bike. I settled on two bungee cords, which I spiral wrapped around the rod case and bike frame. This way I could pedal unimpeded without fear of breaking the rod on overhanging tree branches or narrow passages along the trail.

My neighbor joked with me after she came over to inspect my set-up. She was a mountain biker, too, and not one to hand out compliments, but she praised my innovation: "You've really figured this out," she said. "The Urban Angler — It just looks so, so complete!"

The whole concept of traveling to and from the water on my mountain bike was based on my desire to make my fishing trips an exercise in Sport with a capital S. More than gentlemanly recreation, some people might even describe my idea of angling as "Extreme

Fly-Fishing." I planned to carry my bike and other gear on my back and over my shoulder wherever I had to go to reach fish, meaning whenever I had to navigate around boulders, ford the stream, and hike up, down, or along the steep hillsides that flank Wissahickon Creek.

There was also the opportunity to put personal philosophy into angling practice. I have always experienced a certain, sublime joy in exploring the infinite possibilities found within a fixed space. The 14 iambic pentameter lines of a sonnet, say, or the A B A B rhyme scheme of a lyric poem. Pennsylvania alone has over 10,000 miles of trout rivers and streams within its borders, enough water to keep one angler busy for two lifetimes. I reduced this immense commonwealth of fisheries to the one in my own back alley. I was convinced fish treasure could be found swimming in the depths of the Schuylkill River and Wissahickon Creek.

On Saturday morning I slipped my green khaki fishing vest over my flannel shirt and pulled on my new, knee-high rubber boots. I paused, looked up with closed eyes at the morning sun streaming through my kitchen window, and smiled. All I had to do now was be on my way.

I rode from my Center City row house up to the Philadelphia Museum of Art. From there I headed northwest along Kelly Drive, passed Boathouse Row, passed the Falls Bridge, all the way up to where the Wissahickon flows into the Schuylkill. The first hundred yards of this stretch of the Fairmount Park Bike and Hiking Path is a steep incline that brings the rider over fifty feet above the stream. The view from the summit was impressive: below — a low-head dam, a ten-foot-wide waterfall at its center, mid-stream, plunging white water into a wide pool; behind — a high cliff wet with spring runoff and lush, flowering moss. The territory was familiar now, yet my senses felt something new; I could now approximate the cold rush of the stream flowing around my legs.

I pedaled to the baptismal pool where I had watched the father and son fish the previous Sunday. The spirit was still there in the light and air, but I was alone. My luck could not have been better. The weather was excellent — bright sun, deep blue sky, puffy white cumulus clouds, light breezes — and it was late morning. How I came to

Belmont Pumping Station, b. 1900: a red brick masterpiece, Schuylkill River.

have that special pool to myself at such a prime time can only be attributed to the good grace of Fortune.

A large, uprooted mulberry tree along the bank served as a fine streamside base for my mountain bike, shore lunch, and tackle. I quickly assembled my rod and reel and threaded the fly line and leader through the guides. I already knew which fly I would use: the Muddler Minnow.

A man named Don Gapen first tied the Muddler in 1937. This is a streamer pattern, brown in color, with a short hackle and thick wings close to the body. The fly is designed to resemble a common northeastern freshwater forage fish, the sculpin, although it can be fished weighted like a nymph, or dry to imitate a terrestrial insect.

I first used the Muddler on springtime trout trips during my high school years, and it remains the one fly I can tie with any accuracy. This fact and the fly's consistent effectiveness have endeared it to me, placing it at the top of my list of patterns. My hope was that it would once again be the one to bring trout to my net.

I tied the lucky fly onto the fine end of my tippet using an improved clinch knot, which consists of three to five wraps around the line, followed by pulling the end through the loop that is formed by bringing it back upon itself. Finished, I held the hook flat between the thumb and index finger of my right hand and pulled the line against the resistance of my rod tip until the drag on my reel made a few clicks in reply. I made a ritual of the action to assure myself I was ready.

My first steps into the stream were awkward. Ten years' time had rusted my wading technique. The soles of my rubber boots gripped the rocky streambed well. Still, a few slips had soaked my khakis around the knees by the time I positioned myself at the head of the pool.

All I had to do at this point was cast. Imagine that first kiss with a new lover. The same combination of excitement, apprehension, and passion filled me as I raised my left rod arm, lifted the rod perpendicular to the water, snapped my wrist back, and let the line fly behind me.

Since a fly has no practical weight, the fly caster actually casts the line. The fly rides along for free. The key to the basic backcast is timing. One must let the line roll out just long enough so a second snap of the wrist can bring it forward and place both line and fly flat upon the section of the stream to be fished.

Five or six casts restored my full confidence and some of my old technique. I began to feel comfortable enough to enjoy the view and sounds around me. On my seventh cast I began to contemplate a grackle wandering over some boulders across the creek. These immense metamorphic rocks were some of the valley's signature stone, Wissahickon schist: an attractive building stone with a 550-million-year history. This schist has bands of pink feldspar and milky quartz and flecks of bright mica that add texture and a variation of color within the gray. Smaller specimens are sometimes found encrusted with brown and rust-colored garnets.

The iridescent black bird hopped onto another rock. I saw a metallic flash in the water and heard a strangely familiar sound —

"Thwick!"

Sound and flash coincided with a sudden surge of line through the guides. A deep, forward bend animated my rod. My eyes returned to the surface of the stream as I raised my left arm —

Fish on line!

"Thank you, God!" was what I said.

The water broke, and a small rainbow trout leaped into the air. Success.

I caught and released two rainbow trout during my first hour with the creek. The aerial acrobatics of that species was a wonderful reintroduction to the trout.

I waded back to shore after I released the second fish. I was hungry, and the peanut butter sandwiches and carrot sticks I had brought tasted richer than any peanut butter sandwiches and carrot sticks I had ever eaten. The sun continued to dapple on the surface of the stream, and I found myself happy and lost in a flowing state of no thought, just feeling.

My revelry was mildly interrupted by the sound of wading. A man was moving toward the pool from the riffles below. He was dressed in white sneakers, denim cutoffs, and a flannel shirt. His simple ensemble was topped off with a straw hat that made him look like a postmodern Tom Sawyer. He waved and addressed me with the angler's greeting —

"Catch any?"

"Two trout. My first of the year."

"Good job! This is a great pool. One of my faves."

And with that he made his first cast. He was using ultralight spinning gear to throw a tiny rattling plug.

"And you?"

"I caught one down below. And a bass."

"There are bass in this creek?"

"Yep. Small ones, though. You'll catch lots of sunfish, too. They can get pretty big."

This was great news. I could look forward to a whole season of fishing for a variety of species. I would also have a place to escape from the oppressive humidity that weighs down summer days in Center City.

"Got one!"

He raised his rod as a little fish jumped in the white water across the stream. I slid off the mulberry tree and waded over to him. He brought a feisty smallmouth bass in between us.

"I can catch these guys all day long when it gets warmer," he said while unhooking the bass. "I just walk down from my house on Wissahickon Avenue and wade a mile or two for exercise."

The man continued to work his way upstream as I finished my lunch. When I was done I decided two trout were plenty for one pool. I packed my gear and cycled upstream in search of another spot. I

Free parking, Wissahickon Creek.

passed a long, shallow stretch that offered no visible cover for fish. Nothing grabbed me until I spied a dark green pool flanked by tall trees. My sixth sense whispered two simple words to me—Brown Trout.

I slipped through the wood rail fence and made my descent to the water. This was a very steep grade to navigate, especially with a bike resting on one shoulder. More than once I had to use a fern or a sapling to steady my controlled fall down the hillside.

The pool spoke in a continuous, soft tone as I assembled my gear. I opened my fly box and selected a new Muddler Minnow. The two rainbows had worked over the first one pretty well.

I was alone again, but as I waded into the stream I heard some very cautious footsteps. I turned around and found a large raccoon heading up into the trees. When I paused, she paused, and turned her head. Her masked face stared down at me as if to say: "This is my property, boy. Behave!"

I fished the pool for about an hour with no luck. Frustration began to fill me as evening approached. I was more than satisfied with two trout. Still, a third would be the charm, and I had a real desire to catch a brown, the most fickle of the species.

Rise forms began to break the glassy surface of the pool's tail end as the day began to darken. I crouched down and watched the action.

I guessed two or three fish were sipping insects from the surface. The question was what kind. Right on queue, a single, pale mayfly descended and hovered before my eyes like an advertisement—

Match The Hatch. . . With ME!

I clipped off the Muddler Minnow and looked over my other patterns. One fly stood out instantly—the Light Cahill. This pale, cream-colored dry fly is a highly visible pattern designed to imitate the mayfly of the same popular name. I tied on a size 14 Light Cahill that fairly well matched the size of the living example I had just seen up close.

The day's greatest challenge now arrived. Dry-fly fishing is the most demanding form of the sport. Casts have to have finesse, and pinpoint accuracy is mandatory so flies can float above the fish without any visible drag from the fly line. Even a slight ripple or pause in the float can spook trout, which spend a large part of their lives selectively surface feeding.

My first cast was a disaster that put the rise on pause. I sat on a stone and cursed myself under my breath. The evening air was full of spinning insects. The trout were hungry. And I had to contain myself and wait.

The hatch activity was so heavy that in a short time the trout were compelled to resume feeding. My second attempt with the Light Cahill was much better. I got off a soft cast at my ten o'clock position that landed the fly gently upon the pool. The fly made a slow float toward the tail end riffles until "Slup!"—A take!

The trout darted upstream close enough to the surface for me to see it shaking its head in the struggle to lose my fly. I let the fish take more line as it passed me. The connection was stimulating and physical. This was a weighty fish. It made an arc and swam downstream into the shallows near my position. I stripped in the line as the fish neared. I led it over to a small sandbar behind me where I at last beached the fine brown trout of twelve inches.

Fish continued to rise after I released the brown. Darkness continued to fall, too. I had a long ride ahead of me, some of it along trail that was not lit. The last of my old angling feelings returned: the sentimental sadness that fills me when it comes time to say good-bye to a stream. I rinsed my hands in the cold current and told the Wissahickon I would be back. I packed up and called it a textbook first day on the fly.

Chapter 3

San Juan Worm

The Gifts

My size 12 White Wulff drifted down the middle of a sunny, shallow stretch of the stream. A mottled patch along the tan, pebbled bottom began to cruise toward the surface to meet it. That's when I realized the shape was a large redbreast sunfish guarding its nest. I watched it rise as slowly and as smoothly as an ascending balloon. The fish paused beneath my fly for a brief, final inspection. The moment of decision passed, and the sunny hit. I set the hook and had my first fish of the day.

"There you go, you caught one."

I looked up after I slipped the sunfish back into the Wissahickon. The voice belonged to the fly-fisher who had been wading upstream toward me for the past half an hour. He had been methodically working a shaded section of quiet riffles full of rising trout that had skunked me earlier in the afternoon, and he had been doing so with success. I saw at least two trout make white water at the end of the leader tied to his pale blue fly line.

"The sunfish are rising to dry flies in this pool," I replied.

"I caught a 16-inch smallmouth bass in this pool last year. Right over there—" He pointed to three exposed rocks near the tail end that flowed into the shaded run he had just fished so well. "Bass love to hold around those rocks."

He was a middle-aged African-American man; a well-dressed, well-equipped fly-fisher. He wore a wide-brimmed khaki hat, polarized sunglasses, and a fine set of olive waders. A hardwood catch-and-release net hung from his waist.

"This is one of the best spots for bass in the creek," he said. "You must know how to read the water. Good start."

"Have you fished here long?" I asked.

"Since 1964. Fly-fishing only since 1972—Oh!—A fish just hit my indicator. How about that! Missed him."

He had been making delicate casts the entire time we talked. He was using a weighted nymph, fished upstream. The "indicator" he referred to was a large, bushy dry fly that floated along the surface and served as a bobber for the nymph rolling with the current along the bottom.

"The key is to cast in front of these rocks and make it look so that something good to eat fell off one. Bass love to hang out in the shade and will smack whatever looks like dinner. This is the kitchen."

He retrieved his line with a few quick, smooth pulls and inspected his flies. "Knots! That fish tied me up."

He came closer, using his wading staff to navigate around a group of damp, slippery stones, until he came to a dry boulder at the head of the riffles. He leaned back on it, and I sensed he was offering a silent invitation to engage in conversation. I reeled in my line and waded over to another stone opposite him. A babbling run about one-foot deep and ten feet wide separated us.

"Your form's okay. I could see you're using a medium-action rod. It's a bit stiff."

"Yeah," I agreed. "I could only really afford one rod, so I bought this all-purpose trout and bass model. It's a 5-weight."

He chuckled. "Don't worry about money. We'll get it all. We have you now. Myself: I've got close to a dozen different rods, an antique bamboo pole, and don't forget the flies. We'll have to get you tying soon."

I sat, silent, like a student. I was intrigued by his sudden use of the plural. "I" had become "We," and it seemed as though this man was a fly-fishing avatar sent to welcome me back to the sport. I could tell he could tell I had taken off for a few years to pursue college and career full-time.

"You can never have enough flies. At two bucks a pop, they add up. Trout and trees take 'em on every trip. You've got to tie."

"I plan to, eventually," I said.

He pulled out a sky-blue case from one of his fishing vest pockets and opened it. He tilted the box so I could see its contents. There must have been five dozen flies arranged tightly in rows like hand-rolled cigarettes in a case. I saw more nymphs than I could count, plus dry flies and a few bright, pink, San Juan Worms.

"I dropped a box that wasn't waterproof into the stream once. Took it home and forgot to leave it open to air dry. The next time I went out on the water I found every one of my hooks rusted, ruined."

"What a nightmare!"

"Yes. You don't need a lot of patterns here. This is a caddis stream for the most part. Bring some streamers for bass, some terrestrials in the summer. You can't beat ants and grasshoppers then. Trout love the Sulpher spinners the best, though. Goddamn, they do. I'm thinking of eating one myself to see what the fuss is about."

He thrust his staff into the streambed, pulled himself up, and waded over to me. "Here you go—"

One at a time, he handed me three flies: a bead-head nymph, his take on the American Pheasant Tail Nymph, and a San Juan Worm.

"Use the worm in the spring when the water's roiled. Fish the nymphs in the riffles."

"Thanks," I said. "These are great. I was running low on ammo, you know."

"Get yourself a vise and tie. You'll never run low, and you'll always know you were completely responsible for catching the fish. Just remember they don't belong to you. Let 'em go."

"I always do."

"Continue to; they're a gift."

"You're right."

He checked his watch. "Time to go. My wife's taking me out to dinner. You'll need to get a water-filtration system. You'll get thirsty

Fooled by an Adams: redbreast sunfish, Wissahickon Creek.

here in the summer. And waders, boy! Those knee boots won't do. How do you expect to get at those big bass on the other side of the stream?"

"I'm still in the kiddy pool."

He rinsed his reel back and forth in the stream and turned away toward the opposite shore, talking all the while: ". . . Yep, we've got you now. We'll get all your money, but you won't be sorry. It's a great way of life. It's a way of life . . ."

I waded back to the bank and packed up after he slipped out of view through the trees. I cycled down the bike trail to another stretch of riffles above Valley Green. I walked out onto a flat bar of gravel and cobblestones and set up my tackle beside the creek for another try at the trout. I contemplated my fly options and decided on my new American Pheasant Tail nymph. During the next hour I hooked, landed, and released two trout: a rainbow and a brown.

Chapter 4

American Pheasant Tail

Last Cast

My friendly ex held court every Saturday night while she worked her shift at a fly-fisher's paradise — McGlinchey's Bar. I dropped by for a few pints at the end of a full day of fishing. I recounted my experience on the water, and she rolled her eyes at me from across the booth and pronounced me — "Obsessed."

I disagreed. A healthy enthusiasm may very well appear to be obsession when viewed from the outside. But inside, . . .

. . . On the following Sunday, I was in the middle of hour seven of my fishing trip, with one good rainbow trout to show for the effort. My ankles and left wrist ached from my constant cycling, wading, and casting along the steep terrain of Wissahickon Creek. Rock-hopping in search of trout can do this to the body.

The middle of May weather had been cool, breezy, and primarily gray for most of the day. With evening nearing, the sky was clearing, and the wind was down.

I had been cycling from spot to spot along the small gravel trail that follows the course of the stream, and I now arrived on my mountain bike at a wide stretch of riffles that ran into a slower, narrower, emerald pool. On my side of the bank there was a small, gray stone cabin with "WPA 1938" carved into its cornerstone; purple, yellow, and white wildflowers; catbirds, mallards, and geese.

The stretch of stream was picturesque. A tear-shaped cobblestone bar split the riffles. Shallow and fast on my side, the other was much deeper, owing to the undercut bank at the base of the steep hillside leading up into the trees—

Promising water.

I parked my bike against a sturdy bush, unpacked, jointed up my rod, attached the reel, threaded the line through the guides, and tied on a size 12 American Pheasant Tail nymph. I knew this type of small wet fly would work best given the conditions. I could work it within the white water to resemble a larva, broken free from the bottom, struggling to reach the surface and emerge as an adult caddisfly.

I worked the riffles from the top, down to the fine gravel point of the bar where the other, shallower stretch of fast water joined it to form the emerald pool—

Nothing.

My rubber knee boots crunched the fist-sized stones as I walked back up the bar to the head of the riffles. I tested the clinch knot I had tied and made a short roll cast into the rushing water. My ears and mind both were cleansed as I contemplated the bright, steady, wet sound of the tumbling water. I was together with the stream.

I stripped out the floating yellow fly line and allowed the nymph to wash down much farther than usual. Instead of halting the run at fifteen or twenty feet and letting the fly hang in the current, I continued to strip line and let it work its way down the entire length of steep bank to the tail end of the riffles, which was about forty feet distant. As the nymph neared the end of the fast water—

"Thwick!"—

A hit!—

I struck!—

Fish on line!

A huge trout broke the surface once, twice. I saw the metallic body emerge, then submerge, and I felt the heaviest weight I have yet felt at the end of my rod; like a rock snag, yet pumping with life. The fish made a strong dash up the riffles toward me. The weight of that much heavy fly line alone is formidable in fast water, and now I had the biggest fish of my life added to it.

I waded over the slippery, weed-covered stones in the riffles and around to the calm water along the gravel bank of the bar on my right. I did not want to lose the fish on any near-surface rocks at the head-waters, and I hoped to coax him into the calm, clear part of the pool where I could get a good, close look.

He came, with difficulty, and I saw the full length of him, twice what I had come to expect from a Wissahickon Creek trout. I could tell, too, that he wasn't a young, freshly-stocked rainbow. He was an old brown. His size alone told me he was a holdover that had some-how survived there for three or four years. A middle-aged trout that had competed successfully with hardier bass and sunfish, that had escaped clever raccoons, herons, and the hooks of several—perhaps dozens—of other anglers.

Welcome to Philadelphia! Spring, Wissahickon Creek.

The fish ran back toward the riffles and made a head-shaking half leap once he reached the fast water. Upstream, again, he sped. The sight of him chugging forward against the current, the tenacity of his singular will, impressed me. He was wearing me out. This was hard work. There would be no quick catch.

I did my best to use the leverage of the long rod to pull him out of the riffles, to lead him back in my direction. I unhitched my new,

Thomas Mill covered bridge, Wissahickon Creek.

cherry wood catch-and-release net and pulled him toward it. No way, he swam! He headed out, again, holding me. This was an end game of chess, with stones and stream substituting for black and white squares. I leaned my rod farther to the left, stripped in more line. I could see, at last, the beginning of my clear, tapered leader. I turned him around, back to the shallows, away from the fast water, back toward me. He was getting as tired as me now. I drew him toward my net, closer this time. He made another short run, shook his head, then surrendered. I lifted, slowly, overwhelmed by the shock of his great weight.

He was muscular and richly colored. Red and black spots ran along the length of his old gold sides. The largest trout of my life: 20 inches long; three pounds plus.

I wet my hands and carefully removed the little hook from the bottom corner of his left jaw, felt the cool, heavy thickness of his girth, and revived him. After about a minute together, he swam off, slowly, toward the deep green water.

There was a slow fade to the exhilaration in my mind, an ending akin to the last note of a string quartet. I remained on my haunches for a few more quiet seconds and allowed the feeling to complete itself before I stood up, shook out my net, and reattached it to the rear D-ring on my fishing vest. A mallard family began to work its way single file downstream. Each bird took its turn entering the riffles, slowly speeding up on its way down the natural waterslide.

"Lucky ducks," I said.

Chapter 5

Olive Woolly Bugger

Catfish Friday

Memorial Day Weekend was a washout. Three days of steady rain made it impossible to ride or to fish. The river resembled a coffee with two creamers. I felt the itch to twitch a wet fly more than ever, but I sat in a café and read a book instead.

The following three workdays passed with no rain, light winds. I could wait no longer. Why not fish before work? I figured the Schuylkill River below the falls of the Fairmount Water Works would be running low and clear, the kind of conditions that would give me, a small-stream angler, a fair first attempt at fly-fishing this nearby stretch of wide, big-city water. I set my alarm clock for five a.m.

The early morning streets were clean, quiet, and empty as I rode my mountain bike along the Benjamin Franklin Parkway in the direction of the Philadelphia Museum of Art. On some autumn and spring days there is an exceptionally clear, short-lived quality of light at this time. This was the first day of June, a Friday, and the sky displayed an infinite range of blue. The hues, combined with the deep green foliage and the growing glow on the eastern horizon, gave the city's skyline a sharp, gemlike appearance.

Cardinals, robins, and sparrows began to sing their morning songs. The sound of my bike was low and steady. There was no traffic to drown out these soft sounds; sounds always there, yet frequently underheard.

I merged onto West River Drive a few moments later, passed the PMA, dipped under the Spring Garden Avenue Bridge. To my delight, the river ahead was way down. Several rocky islands dotted the water, and a strip of cobblestones projected ten to twenty feet from the base of the steep green hillside that marked the river's average height. My timing, unwittingly, had been excellent —

It was low tide.

The explorer Arendt Corssen gave the Schuylkill its modern name, which means "hidden creek" in the Dutch language, but what truly remains unseen by most people is the fact that this is a river with a split identity. The neoclassical Water Works, constructed in the Greek Revival style during the 1820s, marks the point where these "Two Schuylkills" segue. Above the falls, it is an inland, freestone river. Below, it is the tidal Schuylkill, part of the Delaware River estuary that drains into the Delaware Bay. The tidal river can rise or fall as much as six or seven feet, depending on the tide. This fluctuation affects the feeding patterns of the fish and makes the biting times more predictable. A greater variety of fish can be found, too, including anadromous species such as eels, shad, and striped bass.

I locked my bike onto the black metal guardrail and hustled down the hillside to the stones: brown, not quite dry, a little slippery. I set up my tackle along a stretch of shore that paralleled a long, narrow island. A swift, smoothly flowing channel separated me from the outcrop. Ducks, geese, gulls, and cormorants were perched there, slowly waking up themselves.

I tied on a size 8 Muddler Minnow and added weight so I could twitch the pattern along the bottom. My first casts targeted the tail end of the channel, where it once again became wide, slow-moving river. Soon after, something weird happened: the fly disappeared! Two or three casts into the fishing I found no fly at the end of my tippet, although a close inspection revealed the knot was still intact. No explanation, strange and frustrating, but the beauty and freshness of my solitary early morning along the river kept my temper in check.

My clear plastic fly box provided me with several other options. I decided on a size 10 Olive Woolly Bugger. This is a dark, fuzzy streamer designed to look like a leech, or a hellgrammite, the larval form of the dobsonfly. I tied it on very carefully and made a few quick casts, again at the tail end—

Nothing.

I walked back over the rocks for about twenty yards to the head of the channel. I stopped beside a willow oak, standing on my left, spreading itself over the water. I made a sidearm cast beneath its branches. The fly drifted back down—

Nothing.

I next made a two o'clock cast in the direction of the island. I let the Olive Woolly Bugger wash down until my fly rod and floating yellow fly line formed a 90-degree angle, then I started to retrieve it against the current, parallel to the bank, along the drop-off that began six or seven feet out. On my first cast I tried an erratic, two fast/one slow retrieve. On the second cast I started to use a slow, steady, swimming retrieve, and tugga-tugga—

Fish on line!

The hard hit occurred twenty feet down from my position, and the fish immediately rocketed toward the outcrop. My rod held weight, heavy, living weight. The weight began to speed up and move upriver in my direction. I stripped in line to keep up, but my rod would not stay high. The fish dove, fast, steady, and strong, headlong into the current.

I began to talk: "If you're a smallmouth bass, you must be just as heavy as the big brown trout I caught two weeks ago!" Next I said: "Are you a striped bass?" . . .

The fish was getting closer to me now, but as it neared shore, Kabooooom!—She reignited. I had to give back every inch of line I had taken. There would be no other way. The bend of my rod resembled the arch of a bridge at this point. The tip dipped into the river! This deep-water battle continued for two or three minutes before I finally got a flashing glimpse of the long, bronze side of a fish just beneath the surface.

"What-Are-You!?!" I wondered.

The fish kept its secret. It dove again, upriver, out of sight. I reminded myself that big freshwater fish tend not to jump. So, I kept

A predatory pose: channel catfish, Schuylkill River.

up, started to strip in line when I could, when she would let me. I prayed my knots would hold. She eventually came back down, hugging the shoreline on my left. The clear leader emerged from the water. I raised my rod tip a little more, and "Howdy!"—I was greeted by an enormous channel catfish.

I netted the big girl and saw my Olive Woolly Bugger lodged snugly in the left corner of her thick upper lip. I dipped my right hand into the river, then carefully grasped her body behind the stiff, potentially dangerous, dorsal and pectoral fins. I unhooked her, lifted her out of the net, and admired her silver gray color, peppered with a few irregular black spots. From her whiskers to her deeply forked tail, she was as long as my forearm and outstretched hand. She began to talk, uttering low, air bladder grunts, reminding me she belonged in the river, not my hand. I recalled the advice from an old wives' tale, kissed her lightly on the forehead for luck, and let her back into the water. She bolted, healthy and strong.

I stood up, happy and successful. The sun rose with me, spilling its warm light over the gold Kasota sandstone of the PMA. Good morning, world. No rain today.

I noticed then that the river was rising, fast. The ankle-deep water had come halfway up the height of my rubber knee boots during the battle. The tide told me it was time to leave. I was happy to go, even though my next destination, after a shower and breakfast, was the office.

Chapter 6

Royal Coachman

Smallmouth Sunday

Here's the story of the big one that came my way . . .

The river was warming from the early June sun, and it was slightly stained from recent rains: ideal conditions for spring bass fishing. I had been spending a Sunday afternoon chasing trout along Wissahickon Creek, but it was two smallmouth bass that had risen to my dry flies, including a spunky, 9-inch fish that did aerial acrobatics in the white water along a bend in the stream. That encounter whetted my appetite for more warmwater action. I packed up early and cycled back toward Center City to the spot along the Schuylkill River I call Ten Rocks.

Ten Rocks is, well, ten rocks: exposed stones ranging in size from an adult snapping turtle to an elephant. The surrounding water holds even more submerged boulders. I had taken note of their positions during low water in the past. These and several tall, modern steel bridges, including one that won a "Most Beautiful" design award in 1960 from the American Institute of Steel Construction, provide the structure that both rock bass and smallmouth bass prefer.

Ten bright, sun-bleached stones could be seen below through the green web of bankside trees and brush. I side-stepped down the hillside with the mountain bike hoisted over my right shoulder, rested it against one of the trees along the shore, and waded out to the first large, exposed rock. I stretched out on it and pieced my rod together and locked my reel into place. Now I needed only ammunition to commence fishing.

I unsnapped my fly wallet . . . Oops! I had only dry trout flies. All of my bass-size streamers and poppers had been left at home. The stretch of river was roiled from a strong, steady breeze, too—terrible dry-fly conditions—but the area looked fishy, more so than at any other time I could remember.

I deliberated my options for several minutes before selecting my largest fly, a size 10 Royal Coachman. This is a nineteenth-century American variation of an antique British attractor pattern, one first tied by Tom Bosworth, an angler who, not too surprisingly, served three British monarchs in the coachman capacity. The Royal has a dark, bushy hackle, white wings, a red silk body, and an orange, black-tipped tail of woodduck feathers.

The classic red and white colors used with bass bugs were present. I could improvise and add a split shot a foot above the fly, which would allow me to fish it wet and deep where the bass might be holding. I could retrieve it in several ways and make it serve as a streamer. This convinced me the Coachman was best qualified to take me were I wanted to go.

The breeze was crisp, even stiff at times. I made a cast down river with the wind and used a quick, darting retrieve, imitating a crippled minnow. On the third pull—Boom!—a smallie hit as the fly passed by one of the snapper-sized stones. He jumped over the rock and did a zig and a zag and two more tail flips before I netted him. Two canoes passed as I played the fish, and the paddlers paused to applaud my success.

This 10-inch fish marked the first time that season the Schuylkill River had offered up a double-digit bass. Until then, the bass I had landed were nine inches or less. These are bass in their second or third year of life; the size bass fishermen refer to as "dinks"—juvenile, "itty-bitty" bass.

Ten Rocks. Summer, Schuylkill River.

Good luck, good air, and adrenaline fueled my mood, which helped me to cope with an immediate angling reality—the spot had been played out—and I was hemmed in close by the high water. The largest of the Ten Rocks were out farther, separated by a maze of little channels that were less than knee deep when the river was at normal flow.

I sat down on one of the smaller stones and watched the river. The water was not at normal flow; the channels were far too high for my rubber boots. So much for the British bankside model of fly-fishing! The Schuylkill, after rain, is not the placid River Test. I thought of the wise fly guy along the Wissahickon, he who had advised me on a previous Sunday to get a set of waders, and I sighed.

Angling is a sport that often calls for improvisation, quick fixes akin to my conversion of the dry Royal Coachman into a makeshift wet streamer pattern. I recalled a recent email from my former college roommate and fishing partner who now lived in Georgia. The two of us used to work around our PSU class schedules in order to wet wade the tiny, unnamed spring creeks that flow throughout that part of Central Pennsylvania. The resurrection of my fly-fishing life had rekindled this dormant corner of our long-distance friendship. His latest piece of brotherly advice reminded me how an angler—a serious angler—has to get wet and dirty to catch fish, especially lunker bass. One has to earn those big fish by getting a few bumps, scratches, and bug bites. Inspired by these words, I took off my boots and socks, rolled up the pant legs, put the boots back on, and waded out. The river was cold and well over the knees. I quickly took on water weight, but once I reached the two largest rocks I took off each boot in turn. Two drains later, and I was ready to angle.

I made two or three casts into the main channel from the second largest stone, a wide riverfront stage just a few inches above the waterline. My Royal Coachman, when I brought it close, looked alluring enough as it moved through the water. It was a small bite for this big water, but fine in terms of color, shape, and action. And, after all, it had already lured one bass.

Another cast hit a snag, one of those light ones that a few careful rod tugs can dislodge. The next was foiled by a gust of wind. I unraveled a small bird's nest from my rod tip and realized I would have to cast between the breezes. This was a simple deduction, but a necessary action if I wanted to cast for distance and accuracy.

My wet trousers chilled my legs while I stood waiting in the breeze. I did a little dance and followed the course of a truck as it passed across one of the two bridges. When the wind waned, I took the opportunity to cast, this time in the direction of the main channel at my three o'clock position. I let the floating yellow fly line run until it was straight, and then began my retrieve. I hit yet another snag fifteen feet out, but this one came alive! The line acquired a will and direction of its own. Fast and deep, the line moved into the main channel. I lifted my rod tip high—

Fish on line!

This one pulled like a bull and stayed deep. I thought I must have hooked into a channel catfish like the one I had caught the Friday before. This fish was fast, though! I pulled to the left as carefully as I could to draw the fish toward the sheltered water between the Ten Rocks. The fish followed, sensed the shallower water, and surfaced.

The gaping mouth of a trophy bass emerged from the river. The image reminded me of a Renaissance woodblock print of a sea monster. The fish shook its head, flashed me the full length of its long, bronze body, and submerged.

"This fish is huge!" I cried. I whooped and hollered like a boy at a football game. "Oh, my God, look at this fish!" I began to intone a short list of names; my fishing companions from the past: "Oh, Alan! If you could only see this fish! Mom! Dad! Stephen! Grandpap! Uncle Herb! This bass is huuuuuge!"

My wrist was working out with a living barbell! I prayed to God for the continued full strength of my six-pound-test tippet. The bass made several of those slow, monumental rises to the surface, the kind that let you see the full, magnificent size, scale, and color of the fish. Life moved at half speed when I saw it fighting. Every detail of fish and water seemed clear and isolated, like the individual stills of a film.

Speechlessness overtook me as I continued to engage the fish. I at last brought her near, alongside the flat stone upon which I stood. I didn't want to lean over and grab her by the bottom lip because the muddy stone was slippery in places. I unhooked my net and led her toward it. This was the key moment. She would either explode again, or surrender. She surrendered.

I raised the dripping net, unhooked the little Royal Coachman that had served so well, then lip-lifted her with my right hand. This was the most magnificent bass I had ever had the honor to hold, a brilliantly colored bronzeback with a glow of green throughout. Her vertical, olive-toned tiger bars were crisply defined.

My reading had taught me that the one large bass among several smaller ones tends to be the mature female. The swollen stomach on this four-pound fish told me she was a mother bass about to spawn. I therefore kept my admiration brief. I cupped my left hand beneath her tail and placed her back into the Schuylkill. I let go her lip, and she shot down into the deep channel.

The sun had reached that point near the western horizon where its color begins to cool. The weekend was coming to a close. I sat on the stones and watched the wind make shifting patterns on the surface of the water. I listened to it sounding in my ears. I said and thought nothing, just listened. I was tempted to keep fishing, but after that fish—

a lunker in any Pennsylvania water, let alone the Philadelphia County stretch of the Schuylkill River—I decided to let the special spot rest. Ten Rocks had given me a trophy of a memory.

Chapter 7

Gray Ghost

A Very Scary Fish Story

City fishing offers a unique set of challenges and possibilities, some fun, some frightening. I experienced one of the latter, a scare of the close encounter kind, near the Water Works one morning.

I arrived along the river at 8 a.m. The Saturday morning scene was sunny, crisp, and calm; white cumulus clouds drifting by; the river at low tide, clear, swiftly moving, accompanied by the white water roar of the falls; exposed stones, smooth, clean, quickly drying to brown in the sun; Baltimore orioles and eastern kingbirds, both singing within the spring green bankside trees.

My eyes couldn't believe it. The clarity, the beauty, the prime water, and there wasn't a single angler there except for myself. I selected a size 10 Gray Ghost streamer and went to play, wet wading the shallows from the falls toward the Spring Garden Avenue Bridge.

The Gray Ghost did not spook the fish. Just the opposite! A breakfast-time bonanza of big bluegills! A pair of fine smallies! A pumpkinseed sunfish colorful enough for an aquarium! Plump, skillet-sized fish all caught and released within view of the Center City skyline.

The fine fishing quickly placed the events of the past night behind me. This put a relaxing, happy end to a nervous mood. You see, the evening before, a friend brought up the arcane subject of dead bodies. What would you do if you found one? What would your first thought be? How would you react? We sat on my stoop under the dim streetlight and offered our answers based on theory and conjecture. The effect of those grim thoughts reached deep inside me and even leaked into my dreams. I later had a nightmare of a woman's voice calling to me from an open grave.

Now that conversation and its unconscious resonation was the last thing on my mind as I reached the wide, shallow channel that separates the riverbank from a long rock outcrop when the tide is low. This is a major transition spot along the river. Midway between the falls and the bridge, this is the place where the swift, shallow water below the falls resumes its sluggish, deeper flow toward the Delaware.

I hiked up the hillside stones to survey the water from above. I always do this, as sometimes fish can be seen holding around rocks and other structure. I found a nice, steady boulder to stand upon and looked down at the channel. I nearly screamed—

I saw a hand!

The pale, bloodless hand was wavering just beneath the clear surface of the channel. It undulated in a slow, dead man motion behind a large submerged stone. I was terrified. A woman had drowned and disappeared in the river a few days earlier while trying to rescue her dog. This was the incident that had inspired my friend's line of questioning. Had some macabre twist of irony brought me to her corpse?

I had to be a good citizen and investigate. I took a deep breath and approached. I felt vulnerable, despite the full, bright daylight. My senses were on guard for dozens of shadowy boogey men and monsters—crazed murderers lurking in the bushes, giant poisonous snakes, man-eating river rats, or simply the frozen, terrified, final expression of the dead woman.

I waded a few feet into the swift water. The current was tough, and it was hard to keep my balance. One thing I didn't need just then was

Redbreast sunfish, Schuylkill River.

to be toppled over, face first, onto a dead body. I shivered with that thought, which almost made the dark image become reality.

I got closer and closer, each step slower and slower, as I progressed into deeper and deeper water. The sun reflecting off the river's surface blinded my eyes. I lost sight of the hand once or twice in the glare.

When I reached the near end of the big stone, I was struck by how much its shape and size reminded me of a casket. I rested my palms underwater against its slimy, submerged edge and leaned over as far as I dared. That's when I saw it —

The hand was actually a white cotton glove! The stone had snagged it at the wrist, and the current had filled the fingers, making it look lifelike!

A very scary fishing spider. Dolomedes tenebrosus, *Wissahickon Creek.*

Chapter 8

Hippie Trout

The channel catfish has played a strong supporting role in the history and folklore of the Philadelphia region. Wissahickon Creek got its name from the fusion of the Lenni Lenape words for "yellow stream" (Wisaucksickan) and "catfish stream" (Wisamickan). Catfish and waffles were the nineteenth century equivalent to the contemporary Philly cheesesteak. Roadhouses lined the Wissahickon Valley at this time, and these served tourists from all over the United States who came to visit the Fairmount Water Works, which was then second only to Niagara Falls as a vacation destination. Fried catfish with relish and waffles awaited them when they returned from their sightseeing.

The Schuylkill's catfish community continued to surprise me whenever I fished the river's tidal section. When the tide was low I found I could angle for Mister and Missus Whiskers using some of the same flies and techniques I used to fish for trout in Wissahickon Creek.

The Schuylkill, at low tide, is a swift river with a cobblestone bottom. The receding tide reveals the river's dynamics—channels, pools, and structure—that are hidden by the flat, featureless water of high tide. Cast upriver at these times and dead-drift a weighted Woolly Bugger or a trout nymph through the channels and around exposed rocks. Catfish will often strike these patterns in the fast water in the same determined way as trout. These fish can be big, too, frequently reaching lengths of twenty inches. The pressure of a fighting, four-pound channel cat has often put an impressive bend in my 5-weight rod, which quickly translates into tired forearms and friction burns on the index finger that controls the drag of the fly line.

Trout nymphs are very effective patterns for channel catfish, perhaps because this species spends so much of its feeding time among the rocks where larval forms of caddisflies, mayflies, and stoneflies cling. A dark pattern like the American Pheasant Tail in sizes 8 through 12 can work well, especially if fished during the low-light conditions when these primarily nocturnal feeders are active.

One late-June evening set these observations in stone. I tied on a size 12 Early Brown Stone nymph, stripped out twenty feet of line, and let the current carry the fly down river. The lights along West River Drive switched on, giving me some unexpected extra light. The rocks that had emerged from the water below the falls were wet and shiny, and I could see the white breast feathers of geese bedding down there for the night. I absorbed the view and let the fly drift in the current until I felt the sharp tugga-tugga strike of a channel cat. My reel began to screech, and the fish happily took me into my Dacron backing before turning and heading back upriver. My manic retrieve to keep up could barely match the swift swimmer. I almost slipped and fell a half dozen times as the fish played me as much as I played the fish.

Once I had netted and released the catfish, I could not help but note the similarities between this experience and that of trout fishing. The conditions of the river, my choice of fly, and the spirited fight of the fish were nearly identical in that dim light to fighting a large brown trout on some wild New England river with an unpronounceable name.

The next day I logged onto the Pennsylvania Fly-Fishing website. Their chat room was always full of brook trout brethren, and even smallmouth bass anglers received a cool "no comment" from some of the purist of the dry-fly purists. Still, I could not help but brag a bit. I also composed an "objective" comparison between channel catfish and trout, which I posted onto the message board:

Trout & Channel Catfish: a comparison

T: Silver gray with black spots
CC: Silver gray with black spots

T: Smooth skin
CC: Smooth skin

T: Prefer clear rivers and streams with rocky bottoms
CC: Prefer clear rivers and streams with rocky bottoms

T: Hit dry and wet flies occasionally
CC: Hit dry and wet flies occasionally

T: Strong, spirited battlers
CC: Strong, spirited battlers

T: Best caught-and-released
CC: Best caught-and-released

The response was large and surprisingly serious. Other fly-fishers came out of their closets and admitted to the serious fun channel catfish had given them in the past. One fellow described how channel catfish hit the surface during the whitefly hatch in late summer. That post received nearly a dozen hits from native trout aficionados who wanted to tackle with something larger than a 7-inch brookie.

The popular notion of the homely scavenger moseying along the bottom of a muddy pond does not apply to the channel cat. *Ictalurus punctatus* is a handsome, muscular fish that prefers clean water and rocks,

Hippie trout! Channel catfish, Schuylkill River.

the structure where its preferred foods—live minnows, snails, and crayfish—abound. Rocks also make convenient holding places for whisker fish during times of high, fast water. These preferences for swift current and live prey make the channel cat the game member of this fish family, which means almost every bass, walleye, and trout angler using lures or flies has had an unexpected run-in with Mister or Missus Whiskers.

Suppose, just for a moment, that the channel catfish has been placed in the wrong family tree. This possibility is all the more likely when one looks at other examples from the world of freshwater fishes. Most anglers know, for example, that the largemouth and smallmouth bass are not true bass at all, but rather the king and queen of the sunfish family, Centrarchidae.

Maybe the humble channel catfish actually belongs in the company of its sophisticated trout companions. Picture a family group portrait: the dainty young brookie in the foreground; the wily old brown in the rear; and in the middle, next to the rainbow, the wild one—the channel cat. Perhaps the whiskers are just an expression of its more relaxed, warmwater lifestyle. Maybe the channel catfish is in fact the hippie trout!

Chapter 9

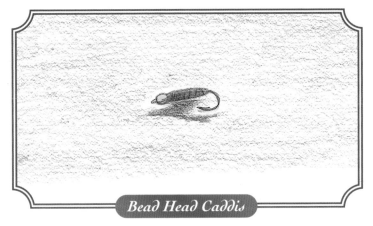

Bead Head Caddis

Night of the White Perch

A depressing low front arrived on the evening of the Summer Solstice. The steel-colored sky reminded me of November. The only difference was the temperature—a comfortable 76 degrees—and the balmy humidity.

The weather complemented the mood. My girlfriend was mad at me. I had canceled a drink date earlier in the week so I could fish the prime time of evening low tide. The next night I had dedicated to a group of new poems. The handwritten manuscripts spread across my living room floor like exposed stones in a stream until there was no more room for her. She retaliated by canceling our Friday night dinner plans.

I rang her buzzer after work the following afternoon. She came down and frowned. "TGIF!" I beamed. "Have you changed your mind?"

"No! Find something else to do!" were her first, and last, words of the day.

What to do? I turned away from her slammed door and walked home, whistling, hands in pockets. What to do? An easy answer—

I packed my fishing gear and cycled to the Schuylkill River.

When I got to my spot the surface of the water was dark, smooth, and strangely quiet, just like me. Then a staccato wind began to blow from the southeast after I set up along the stones below the Water Works. The gusts effectively knotted my first two casts. Two horrendous bird's nests forced me to tie on two different leaders during the first half hour of fishing. Was this my comeuppance? The conditions were the most challenging I had ever faced. I was having a day of it— Chaos on all fronts.

I scanned the water after I finished my third leader, tippet, and fly. The wind had abated during my tie, and the river had turned into liquid glass, its colors ranging from the deepest greens to the darkest grays. What looked like raindrops began to roil a section of the river to my right. The disturbance moved upriver toward my position. As it closed in I realized the surface was peppered by dozens of minnows breaking the water.

This was a sure sign that a larger species was feeding from below, taking the opportunity to fill up during the calm before the rain. I guessed the mystery fish might very well be striped bass.

I had plenty of room to cast for distance. The tide was low, and I had a wide expanse of smooth stone on which to stand beside the water. I made three false casts before sending off a solid thirty feet of fly line and leader toward the commotion.

I stripped the fly across the surface in the same rapid, anxious manner as the minnows. A hard hit smacked my fly in the middle of the maelstrom, and a bright silver flash sounded. The taker made tight circles that constantly required me to readjust my rod position in order to keep the line taut.

A moment later I landed a plump, silver, 10-inch fish. What was this? The fish had been a quick, head-shaking battler, and it resembled some of the ocean species I had caught while pier fishing along the Atlantic coast, fish such as spot, or croaker. It had the same flat, pelagic shape, and a handsome silver color with faint horizontal stripes above the lateral line. Too small to be a striped bass, it turned out the Schuylkill had given me a new species I had never caught before—white perch.

The fish in my net caused a synchronicity. A friend had recently given me one of her cookbooks, A. J. McClane's *The Encyclopedia of Fish Cookery*. I had read her gift from cover to cover during one rainy weekend, and I now recalled the entry for white perch, one the most influential fish in the history of Philadelphia, and America.

If we reel back the clock to 1732, we'll see the formation of The Schuylkill Fishing Company; a club devoted to the arts of angling and hunting, the first club of its kind in the world. The white perch was then as important a food fish to the region as striped bass and American shad, so much so that the club incorporated three white perch into its own flag of state. The club was loyal to his Majesty, King George III, but the war for independence changed everything. George Washington and French General Lafayette came to dine in the club's Fish House beneath a new red, white, and blue flag that featured the silhouette of a white perch surrounded by 13 stars.

I released my first perch and saw minnows again, this time fleeing an otherwise calm-as-glass eddy above the willow oak where I had caught my first Schuylkill channel catfish. I hiked down to the tree and made a sidearm cast into the bubbling pool of frantic little fish. Two quick strips of my Muddler Minnow brought on another "Smack!" I saw the silver flash and felt another tenacious battler at the end of my line. I soon brought a second white perch to my net.

A storm front quickly soaked up the sky space over Center City. The Philadelphia Museum of Art and the temples of the Water Works betrayed their classical forms and acquired a gothic cast in the dimming light. I threw my fly back to the hot spot. The wind picked up during my retrieve and began to blow in the kind of gusts that make fly-fishing impossible. I could not keep my rod from bending to the will of the shifting wind. I reeled in automatically, but not before a smallmouth bass made a manic little run for my fly. I brought the bright little bronzeback to shore and quickly returned him to the river.

The air cleared and the temperature dropped within minutes. Calm returned as a great silver, white, and lead-gray tempest passed overhead. The center was spinning in slow motion, opening like a funnel cloud at the moment of its conception. Tendrils of cloud unfurled

A portrait of the poet's fishing pole, Schuylkill River.

and undulated like an immense jellyfish. I hunkered down, looked up into its eye, and said: "Hi!"

It responded peacefully, passing by without opening the flood-gates. I stood up from my crouched position, rod in hand, a solitary fish-shaman.

I moved my mountain bike up to the brush line and worked my way to the falls of the Water Works. By nine o'clock I had added a small channel catfish to my catch list, but no more white perch. I paused in the growing darkness to watch a great blue heron fish for minnows along the stretch above me.

The lights along West River Drive switched on at nightfall, instantly illuminating the white water of the falls. The heron flew off upriver, leaving me alone. With the lights on I could see well enough again to tie knots. I opened my fly wallet and noticed one of my bead-head nymphs, though designed to resemble a caddis pupa, bore a passable likeness in shape and color to the minnows that had been

Summertime skyline view, Schuylkill River.

jumping earlier. Improvisation again. The white body and flash of the bead in a darting retrieve would look like hapless prey. My gears began to turn. Striped bass are nocturnal and love to follow the baitfish that congregate in areas lit by streetlights. Might the white perch share this habit? These two fish are first cousins in the Percichthyidae family.

I tied on the nymph and positioned myself beside the edge of the river. I saw the faint outline of a submerged outcrop of rocks about twenty feet distant. I cast the weighted nymph so it would flow past the eddy behind the outcrop. On my first cast—

Fish on line!

The streetlights allowed me to see the silver flash of fish that my left wrist could feel moving upriver at high speed. The perch made short run after short run, each one spiraling up my level of delight, as the fish continued its attempt to shake the hook. When I lifted the perch from the river I became a boy again; I was standing on a pier along Virginia Beach, night fishing when the school was in, the tide was out, and the bite was on fire.

I caught 13 white perch in a row. One after another smacked my nymph, and each one fought like a bluegill with booster rockets. I was smiling now, the sky had cleared, and the night was filled with stars. A romantic Friday night with Milady was not meant to be. This was the night of the white perch.

Chapter 10

Woolly Worm

A River Revival

T he great blue heron stood on a boulder like a fisherman dressed in faded denim. As tall as a small man, the bird lifted one of its slender legs and took a slow, careful step over the swift currents flowing between the stones. Like me, this angler preferred to fish during low tide, the time when the river allowed itself to be read.

I dismounted from my mountain bike and locked it onto the guardrail along the bike path. Instead of hoisting myself over, I slipped through, so I would not disturb the bird until I had at least snapped a photo. Herons are solitary, fishing birds, and like most fishermen spook at the slightest sign of an approach.

I crouched behind a patch of blooming purple thistle and white Queen Anne's lace and snapped two photos. I felt like an intruder in one respect because to reach the water I would have to stand and climb down the rocks on the hillside directly above the bird's bankside perch. I watched it watching all until the urge to fish returned to me. I stood; it took off. The bird flapped its wings in almost slow motion, then glided over the water to another outcrop of rocks in the middle of the river.

The Saturday morning sun was already high and bright and hot. The light and heat baked the boulders dry moments after they had emerged from the receding tide. I made my way along the bank, over and around the stones, and stopped thirty yards down river where a large catalpa tree spread itself over the river. A fat lead sinker hung from a length of monofilament off one of the tree's middle branches. It made strangely compatible company with the catalpa's green bean seedpods. The weight served also as a warning; my casts would have to be precise and low to the water.

The tree's shade cooled the back of my neck, and the shifting patterns of light and dark on the drying stones reflected the liquid clarity of the early morning air. This was the spot. Here, beneath this tree, was a crescent-shaped eddy about thirty feet long and fifteen feet wide. A broken trail of foam wound its way toward me in a slow, clockwise motion that led back to the main channel flowing on my left. I could feel a quiet area full of food for feeding fish.

I assembled rod, reel, line, and leader and positioned myself behind the cover of a waist-high boulder that broke the current at the head of the eddy. This spot contained textbook conditions for smallmouth bass, so I tied on a large Woolly Worm and cast it toward the tail end where two rocks, dark and damp, stuck out from the busy surface.

My retrieve commenced as soon as the wet fly hit the water. Bass often strike out of reflex, and a dead fly is just another bit of flotsam going by on the river as far as this particular species of game fish is concerned. The most important thing for a river bass angler to do, after an accurate cast to a spot that may hold fish, is to make the lure look alive.

The retrieve was slow and steady, a regular rhythm that allowed my concentration to appreciate the tower of City Hall and its colossal bronze statue of William Penn rising with the rest of the Philadelphia skyline in the distance. The fact that I could fish for smallmouth bass, the silver medallist on the freshwater fly-fisher's podium, and that I could do so so close to the city, was an epiphany of sorts. The Schuylkill River and its ecosystem, once polluted and near death, had endured and transcended the burden of sins placed into it for the sake of industrial, urban, American development. And here, for one citizen of Philadelphia, was the proverbial silver lining.

A sharp tug brought my full attention back to the river. I raised my rod and felt living weight. This was not a rock snag. My floating yellow fly line became straight as the taker sounded into the channel on my left and began working with the current, which instantly doubled the weight bending my fly rod—

Fish on line!

I lifted both arms above my head and held my rod parallel to the river to let the fish take as much line as it wanted. Twenty feet later, it curved back toward me. I quickly took in the slackening line, raised my rod to an 80-degree angle. The fish felt my presence leading it off course, and it took off a second time. Two sharp tugs forced me down with my rod. The water broke, and a healthy smallmouth bass danced on the river within a shower of sun-bright droplets.

The bass further complicated my catching it by sounding again toward the submerged rocks along the bottom. It sped behind the river side of the waist-high boulder. Fine tippet material frays easily on these rough chunks of stone, and the bass perhaps knew this from previous experience. I leaned over the rock and could see down to the length of it, head yanking hard in both directions, doing its best to shake the hook and get under cover.

The fish was tiring now, enough to let one arm hold both rod and bass at bay while I unhooked my catch-and-release net from a loop on my fishing vest. I stood back, crouched down, and led it over toward the mouth of the net. Not quite! It made one last dash of six or seven feet before turning over enough to allow me to net it.

I took a quick photo of the fish spread out on the wet black mesh of the net, then lip-lifted it to unhook the fly. Thumbing the bottom lip and holding the fish face up and vertical can calm bass. I did this, and the bass relaxed, but I was upset to see the sight of blood. The hook of my fly had set inside its mouth, beside the fish's tongue, and it must have hit one of the tiny arteries in and around its gills. I used my forceps to remove the fly quickly and cleanly, but when I placed the bass back into the sheltered water along the bank a small, translucent cloud of blood puffed out of the fish's mouth and dispersed with the current. The fish floated up and turned on its side.

A Philadelphia native: largemouth bass, Schuylkill River.

Yearling smallmouth bass by Boathouse Row, Schuylkill River.

I have always practiced catch-and-release as a golden rule, and have always prided myself on quick, clean releases of my catch, but this fish was in trouble. It had lost blood and had gone into shock.

This was early July—bass season—so it was legal to keep the fish if it was at least a foot long. I quickly measured the bass from head to tail: eleven inches. I was now facing the ethics of angling.

I decided I was neither going to keep nor give up on this beautiful bass. I began to do what I knew I could do. I first had to get the fish breathing again before its heart stopped. I righted it, turned it around, and holding it with both hands, placed it face first into the current. This way water could pass through and aerate its gills. I pushed it forward and back, too, the equivalent of fish CPR.

Two or three minutes of this action brought positive results. The bass would no longer list in the water, and its gill flaps opened and closed, albeit slowly. I next lowered it to the bottom, to a depth of two feet. The added water pressure helped the bass regain its equilibrium. I let it go and the fish held itself steady on the bottom. Its full, mottled bronze coloration had returned.

"We're two thirds of the way there!" I said.

The third and final phase of recovery involved a combination of everything I had done up to that point, plus facing it back into the full force of the main current. I guided the fish underwater around some submerged stones into a swift, narrow channel flowing behind the big boulder and rocked it back and forth along the bottom. I did this for another minute before leading the bass back to the head of the eddy where it first hit. I let go, and this time the fish bolted forward into the deep water, tired, but certainly vigorous enough to fend for itself once again.

I took a break and walked back with my camera toward the falls where another angler had since taken up a position. He was drifting minnows beneath a float for channel catfish.

"Any luck?" he asked.

"Yes," I said.

Chapter 11

Hornberg

The Trio

P oet, outdoorsman, editor—Edgar Allan Poe combined his inter-
ests and explored Wissahickon Creek during his years in
Philadelphia. He made numerous hikes and rafting adventures along
its way, one of which he recorded in a piece of prose published in
1844.

"Morning On The Wissahiccon" describes his vision of a great elk.
The reader witnesses the apparition within a mystical, Poe-etic land-
scape of mossy boulders and placid tarns until the poet delivers one of
his classic twists: the elk turns out to be a very real animal grazing
along the stream, and a very domesticated one tended by a master.

Poe's lush, bucolic description of the precipitous Wissahickon
Valley continues to hold true, especially during the deep green days of
high summer. The heavily forested gorge and the stream's steep
descent keep the creek's waters cool enough to support a year-round
trout fishery, and though no wild elk are to be found drinking from

the stream at dawn, a wide variety of migratory and permanent bird life can be seen and heard morning, noon, and night.

I found a series of three long pools on an early August afternoon. The day was gray and misty, making the rich green hillsides a shade darker than if bathed in full sun. A bone-toned dead tree, softened by the haze, stood like an impressionist totem halfway down this stretch of the stream, a scene that could have come from the brush of French Symbolist painter Odelon Redon.

A great blue heron slipped into view downstream by the time I had assembled my gear and waded myself into the Wissahickon. The bird perched on a wide boulder that sloped into the stream. A tilt of the head, a bend of the neck, and a patient series of steps at five-second intervals brought the big bird to the water's edge.

I made a delicate first cast and let my Hornberg wet fly roll down back to me. The Hornberg is an interesting fly—a streamer with a distinctive striped body of jungle cock feather and a dry-fly hackle—first tied by a Wisconsin conservation warden named Frank Hornberg. A small redbreast sunfish hit the pattern, and I played the spirited yearling to my feet.

I kneeled on a dry stone to unhook the sunfish and caught a bright flash out of the corner of my right eye. I looked up and saw the heron with a long silver fish—a trout—firmly gripped in its bill. The bird made a heavy leap across the stream onto the gravel bar along my side. It flipped the trout around with one quick motion and swallowed the fish, headfirst.

I carefully waded to a group of large stones at the head of the heron's pool and made a short roll cast into the headwaters. I had a strong strike during my retrieve, and a smallmouth bass surfaced, shook its head, and headed downstream. The heron caught site of our motion, flew to the tail end, and resumed fishing.

The dark bronze bass surfacing before me was one of the stream's true natives. It must be admitted that the majority of the Wissahickon's trout are stocked, although there is limited reproduction of brown trout from those that are holdovers, or gravid—full of eggs—a condition that occurs occasionally within the population of fall stocked fish. The creek's entire smallmouth population sustains

Smallmouth bass, Wissahickon Creek.

itself in the stream, which produces a most challenging quarry. The average 10-inch fish has survived the heron, anglers, and competition from trout for two or three years.

I netted the bass and heard a sharp "Chica-Chica-Chica-Chica" from above as I unhooked the Hornberg. A male belted kingfisher came swooping down the pool in my direction like a jet on a strafing run when I raised my gaze. It alighted on the dead tree and called again, apparently trying to flush the heron, or me, or to tell us both that this end of the pool belonged within its territory.

"Chica-Chica-Chica-Chica," the kingfisher called. I released the bass, which dove for its submerged boulder, and I remained low on my own. I had never seen a kingfisher in the wild before and was more than curious to study its fishing style.

It didn't take long to learn. The bird dive-bombed, face first, into the shallow side of creek. Its all-American red, white, and blue form burst forth a moment later in a second shower of spray. It flew back to the same branch from which it launched itself, a minnow now it its bill.

The irony of this moment delighted me. Here was the stealth strategy of the heron, the direct aerial assault of the kingfisher, and the tool-using tactics of my own species. We were a trio of successful fishers, yet, for all of my equipment and study, I was not the one to catch the trout. Instinct had soundly defeated reason. Wings had won, hands down.

Sunday morning near Green Lane. Summer, Wissahickon Creek.

Chapter 12

Fat Brown Pigskin

Fat Brown Pigskin

The classic fish story has always taken its cue from the tall tale. Hyperbole is mandatory: the conditions are always challenging, bad weather is looming, night is falling, and the fish are as cunning as they are huge.

As September arrived, I found myself torn on Saturday mornings between my love of Penn State college football and my love of Philadelphia fly-fishing. Football often won the coin toss. Still, during one half time, I took a break from my winning alma mater and let my angling imagination run with the ball . . .

Fat Brown Pigskin
by
F. L.Y. Linebacker

I once spent a particularly aggravating—and fishless—morning and afternoon along Wissahickon Creek. Not a single rise, not even a sunfish. I cursed myself. I had sacrificed a full

Saturday of college football and fattening snack food for a day of fly-fishing with no angling reward.

The majority of this particular stream flows within the boundaries of a state park. A gravel hiking path follows the length of the creek, and many couples walk their dogs along it on weekends. They sometimes toss balls into the water below for Fido to fetch, and sometimes these get swept up by the current and lost.

Well, I found one of these along the bank—a football—a peewee leaguer about half the size of regulation pigskin. The ball had come to rest beside a stretch of riffles I reached around dusk. My tired mind finally stopped listening to my nagging empty stomach and began turning over an idea . . .

I searched my fishing vest for the biggest hook I had with me—a size 2/0 that could have ended up as a streamer for large striped bass—and I tied the football onto this with some

Wissahickon schist formations, Wissahickon Creek.

large striped bass—and I tied the football onto this with some spare, six-pound monofilament.

I contemplated my new creation. It was a bit big for the stream and did not match any particular hatch, but large attractor patterns often bring bites from big fish. Confident, I attached it to the fine end of my tapered leader. Rig set, I waded into the middle of the riffles and made a fabulous, 50-yard cast upstream so the football would pass the big log resting along the undercut bank of the creek.

The football rolled with the current, spiraled along a swift, narrow channel toward the log. Suddenly, the water broke! There was a terrific swirl, and the football got sucked under with a heavy wet "SLAP!" sound that resembled two massive linemen colliding on rain-soaked turf.

Interception!

My reel screamed as the fish made a mad downstream sprint with the ball. My long pole doubled over. For thirty minutes I played the tenacious giant as it swam around midstream boulders like a tailback chugging around linebackers toward the goal line.

And you know what?

I scored! A 33-inch, ten-pound brown trout! The fish was a beauty, a true trophy, but I earned an extra point for releasing it back into the stream unharmed.

I have since christened my new fly pattern the Fat Brown Pigskin. It's a sure-fire fly for lunker trout in the fall!

The Fat Brown Pigskin

Hook: Heavy wire, long shank, size 2/0.

Thread: 6-pound-test monofilament, or any darn string you have handy.

Body: Peewee League pigskin, inflated fully.

Chapter 13

Adams

Fishing Without A Net

You have to let go, no matter how well the well-earned treasure may hold you. A trout, a fishing trip, a life experience: all mark transitory stretches of time that pass into memory. The moment flows as the stream flows . . .

. . .The inevitable losses, the partings that occur from time to time, become more bearable when lived within a stream of thought and action. This is not giving up the ghost; this is giving to the spirit. Chance is engaged, possibilities are modulated: an individual finds a more desirable life and then pursues that way.

Consider this case — the fall of all fishers — the knowledge, the sadness, the sense of loss that comes when we cannot return a fish alive to its own stream. Nearly every angler has had to deal with the little panfish that has gobbled the hook and begun to bleed from its gills, or has seen the funerary float of the dead catfish down the river, the same fish you yourself handled too roughly half an hour earlier.

Fishing for sport, like all outdoor activities, brings with it an internal debate. The angler pauses —

Do I do harm to the environment?

The answer is, of course, subjective and varies from person to person. Some fly fishers are catch-and-release and use barbless hooks and underwater resuscitation techniques. Other anglers yank out anything that swims and will keep every fish they land, even if the size or numbers both defy legal limits.

How to learn from and live this life, yet let go of the guilt that sometimes accompanies the consequences?

A simple way to tackle this issue is to practice catch-and-release, both as a style of fishing and as a way of life. Letting the other go allows life to be lived in the flowing moment, which make the partings less "temporary pain" and more "lasting pleasant memory" for the one. Fisher and fish together are better for it when both part as equal partners.

Studies of catch-and-release methods have yielded enough data to show that fish mortality remains low if the angler makes a clean, gentle, and quick release. An angler should play the fish quickly and as gently as possible. Move with the force of the fish you have hooked, and the more quickly and humanely and gamely will be the match between fisher and fish. Hooks should be extracted with wet hands and forceps, which provide safe, surgical hook removal. Another excellent tool to facilitate this process, one that prevents a fish from being dropped or otherwise injured, is a good net.

I was wading along a wide pool below the Walnut Lane Bridge. The bright yellow leaves of tulip trees decorated the brown, rocky bottom of the creek. The sky above the tinted canopy was high and blue, the air crisp and almost cold. I had this and the entire stretch of stream to myself on a perfect Monday afternoon in early October.

Standing, midstream, I cast my Adams dry fly along a high cut bank shaded by late season wildflowers. This course floated the fly into a small eddy. The fly traveled on a leisurely route until a dark form rose from below and softly met it. The take was as gentle as a handshake.

The fish gave me a strong tussle, but did not jump. I brought her near and saw the black spots and silver sides of a healthy female brown trout, perhaps gravid. I led her to my net and lifted her out of the creek.

The Adams neatly lodged in the upper left lip fell out on its own when I let the leader go slack. The fish was calm enough for me to use my damp forearm as a measure: a few millimeters short of a foot.

I lowered fish and net into the water, oriented the trout with the current, and let go. The fish returned to its corner of the pool before I finished counting to three.

I shook off my hands and stood, contemplated the canopy of trees, listened to the subtle, soft language of the smoothly flowing stream. A few bright, red maple leaves parachuted down to me as I watched a distant jet make a vapor trail.

I waded out of the creek with my fly rod in hand and headed downstream along the bank. My shore lunch was waiting. I could already taste the full harvest flavors of peanut butter and apple butter mixing in my mouth.

The sound of my hungry stomach could not drown out a little voice that began to whisper in my mind. Something was wrong. Something was not right. I felt too light. What was the matter? I wondered and continued hiking along the bank carpeted with leaves until I realized my steps were no longer accompanied by the regular, reassuring bump on the right thigh that came from my swinging—

"Net!"

My cherry wood catch-and-release net was gone! I swung around in horror. I must not have reattached it to the D-ring on my fishing vest. The brown trout and the yellow and red foliage had seduced me so completely that I had let go of my—

"Net!" I cried. "Here, Net!"

The riffles were free of debris and shallow enough that I could have seen the net's blond wood frame had it caught onto a projecting stone. I looked and looked, calling and calling out to my net as if it were a pet—

"Net!"

Nothing.

The net might have floated down and lodged itself along the next bend if it had somehow made its way through the riffles, and apparently it had. I hiked as fast as I could to that deep pool. A spring washed the face of a small cliff on the far side that bordered the creek. The smooth line where the gray wet stone met the emerald water was not interrupted by the castaway body of my—

Urban solitude. Autumn, Wissahickon Creek.

"Net!"

I waded along both banks from the riffles to the deep pool and back again. Every empty nook, cranny, rock pile, and logjam left me more and more disheartened. The last rays of sun began to fade from the very tops of the tallest tulip trees. By then my net was well on its way to the sea.

Packed, sans net, I ascended the steep bank on the trailside of the creek. My thighs burned from both the hike up and the heavy bike and tackle balanced on my shoulders. When I reached the top I looked back down and contemplated the Wissahickon's waters, searching the surface of the creek in precise sections like a spy satellite. I saw leaves, logs, and stones, but no sturdy net.

First stop on the way back, Wissahickon Creek.

I mounted my bike, said good-bye, and headed home. I pictured my net, cold and alone, drifting in the dark water of the stream. No longer would it spend its off hours hanging from the handlebar of my mountain bike in my apartment. No longer would it match my khaki pants and fishing vest as I struck a streamside pose. And I would be incomplete, missing a little part that had become me.

The ride back to Center City cleared and redirected my mind. Thoughts stopped drifting and began to focus on a new image, a more positive possibility: maybe some youngster, some boy or girl fishing with Daddy, would find the net the next day—

"Daddy! Daddy! Look what I found!"

"Cool!" Daddy would say, taking the net and shaking it dry. "That's treasure! I'll take care of it for you until your old enough to use it!"

"Thanks, Daddy!"

My loss would end up as the gain of some other angler, maybe even a child. That scenario made me smile.

Night was falling fast on the final stretch of my adventure. I chased the rising moon and ruminated. The day had again come down to the last cast, and luck had allowed me to come out even. My last cast had taken my net, yet had given me a brown trout. I had lost my net, yet found myself singing one of my poems along West River Drive as I approached the bright lights of Boathouse Row and the red, white, and blue Philadelphia skyline—

The thinnest slice of waxing moon apostrophes
The salmon, sun-setting sky.

The waning day gives way to the night.
The question now must be why:

Why the growing depth of darkness
When color is in supply?

The thinnest slice of waxing moon apostrophes
The salmon, sun-setting sky.

Epilogue

Popper

Parallel Lines

Sit beside the stream,
Write about your life . . . .

My mother's mother's maiden name was Miller. I believe I acquired my passion and gift for fishing from this one of the four main branches of my family tree.

I have a romantic image of an early Miller, dressed in the Germanic peasant costume of the something-teenth century. Finished grinding salt and barley for the day, I see him take his long willow pole a few pools upstream. There, resting on a sun-bleached boulder, he spends a quiet afternoon catching wild, foot-long brown trout on angleworms. The *Salmo trutta*, roasted, make a flavorful addition to his family's simple meal of bread, eggs, and cheese.

My first fishing memory involves my father's mother and my twin cousin. I called him my twin then because he was born just a week before me and was the closest person I, an only child, had to a best friend and sibling until I reached grade school.

We were four years old. Grandma Swegman had bought one of those molded plastic spincasting combos that are more toy than fishing outfit. This one was an all-American red, white, and blue. She took us to the Boathouse end of North Park Lake, a 74-acre, horseshoe-shaped impoundment located a few miles north of Pittsburgh, the city where I was born and raised. We had a shore picnic and took turns using the rod. I think we used canned corn, suspended beneath a bobber the size of a baseball, for bait.

No fish were completely fooled by us that afternoon, but my cousin did get a bite. He was so excited and proud when his mother continued to repeat: "You got a bite! You got a bite!" all the way to the car. I got skunked, and I guess the sunken feeling showed on my face. Grandma Swegman, always a positive reinforcement in my life, refused to see me let down: "There was a big fish swimming around your bobber," she said. "I saw him—a big trout—swimming around your bobber."

The destination of my first real fishing trip was North Park Lake, too: the opposite, wilder end where weed beds and overhanging trees lured only serious anglers. I was six, and my mother's father and my godfather were my guides.

Grandpap had taught me about tackle, bait, casting, and hooking fish earlier that particular spring. He would run his thick pink fingers through his thin white hair and show me, with infinite patience, how to tie knots. He also expected me to study at home, giving me his antique copy of a Golden Guide, *Fishing*, for me to read. I contemplated the pictures of tackle, rigging, and fish for hours during the weeks leading up to the opening day of trout season. I internalized the lines and lingo so deeply that acrobatic rainbows and stealthy browns filled both my day and night dreams.

My grandpap and godfather were serious fishermen who followed a ritual I was to know well. They always woke with the four a.m. darkness. I only pretended to wake with them that first morning, due both to my grandpap's snoring and my overactive, insomniac's imagination that played out dozens of different fish-filled scenarios.

We packed the car with a silent quickness, ate a simple breakfast bowl of warm oatmeal, and "hit the road" to the lake at a time when ours was the only car driving up the normally busy McKnight Road. We arrived lakeside in the low light of an April dawn. Mist rose from the calm water as thickly as from the surface of a steaming pot. We three swished through the deep green, dew-covered grass to the shore, the occasional "clink!" or "clunk!" of our shifting tackle our only other sound.

We had won. We were the first fishermen along the lake. My contained excitement erupted in a manic burst of youthful efficiency. I assembled my rod and tackle and baited up before either of them had tied on their hooks. I cast out and shivered with excitement at the sight of the splash my bait made as it entered the lake. No more false casts into the backyard grass. I was fishing for real.

I had to use redworms — "beginner bait" — although I was prevented from using a plastic bobber hanging from a V of line between two guides of my rod. "Floats make fishing too easy, or else make lazy fishermen," I was told. My attention instead focused on the fine end of my rod and the length of line leading into the water. I was waiting for that little tug at my rod tip, the curls of monofilament stretching taut, signaling life on the other end. By definition this was still fishing, yet my mind was always in motion, paying close attention for life animating my line.

No more than a minute could have passed before I received my reward: more than a nibble, a strong strike! I lifted my little spincasting rod from its forked stick holder and set the hook. That tug became attached! The rest of the world condensed and focused into the field of view before me as I reeled in the moving weight, saw a small splash disturb the placid, misty surface of the lake. The fish zigged and zagged, and I reeled in line, continued reeling . . .

I pulled a pan-sized bluegill out of the water. I instantly fell in love with the fish's handsome blue sides and burnt orange belly. I swung my upheld rod and fish to my left and saw my grandpap on the other side of the picnic table, pausing for a second to smile. He nodded to my godfather, who was lost in the intricacies of a knot. He looked over his left shoulder and joined him with a grin: "It didn't take him long at all, did it?" he asked rhetorically.

I received my first fly rod on the day I graduated from eighth grade. That sunny June morning had been at first very sad for me. I was filled with 13-year-old nostalgia and memories that, while not old, were already known in my mind as the one and only sure thing I would take with me when the ceremony was over. I knew many of the faces I had spent eight years with would disappear forever after that morning. So strong was this feeling of impending loss that I even shook hands and made friends with my long-time nemesis just before I left the schoolyard of St. Peter's parochial for the last time. This was an ironic moment. I had been the one child who did not cry in that very schoolyard on the first day of first grade, and here I was, eight years later, leaving as a sad young man.

The feeling did not last. My stepfather had a surprise prepared for me: a 5-weight fly rod and reel combo, complete with a selection of his own flies and poppers. I had indeed graduated—to the most refined fishing style.

He took me that afternoon to Lake Arthur, a trophy bass lake an hour and a half north of Pittsburgh. We fished a cove covered with lily pads. To make it even more of a challenge, we fished from a canoe. I later realized my stepfather was teaching me two of the key elements of fly-fishing: accuracy and balance. Lily pads are a challenging form of cover, easy to snag upon, but rewarding to the accurate caster because big fish love to rest beneath these small, natural parasols. Float fishing low to the water requires a smooth ebb and flow of casting motion— balance—in order for the boater(s) to stay steady and dry.

I fast learned a successful, standard backcast and roll cast within these constraints, and I was soon placing my popper on or near lily pads, casts that one or two short pulls later often drew a hit from a big bluegill, pumpkinseed sunfish, or plump yellow perch. My stepfather caught these and big largemouth bass on deer-hair bass bugs. We caught and released fish until it was too dark to see our lines.

My fly-fishing passion was born.

My other passion, creative writing, developed at the pace of a lazy southern river. There were many bends and eddies along this path, yet each one carried me forward toward that infinite sea of possibility that is poetic language.

Lincoln-Douglas debate and extemporaneous speaking exposed me to a variety of magazines and newspapers during high school, and I knew by my senior year that I would study journalism at the university. The image of the print reporter inspired me. Here was a person, a professional, who could participate in his or her diverse interests through observation, investigation, and writing. That breadth appealed to me. I passed the writing test to join *The Daily Collegian* staff at the end of my freshman year and was assigned to the Arts beat.

Writing about the Arts brought me to poetry, specifically the work of Keats, Yeats, Rimbaud, and Poe. Reading influenced writing, and my own took on an added dimension when I began to write poetry between the spring semester and summer session of my sophomore year.

I had missed the first full month of that particular trout season because of my full-time studies and long hours as the new Assistant Arts Editor. I had applied myself very hard during my second year. I had studied the Japanese language, started the course work in my new double major of Art History and Print Journalism, and made the dean's list.

When I arrived home at the end of that busy spring semester, my stepfather could tell I had a space inside me that needed to be filled—with fishing—and a need to release something indefinable locked inside me. On a gray weekday during intercession, he took a day off, and we drove to Somerset County to a stream where I had spent many days during my high school years: Laurel Hill Creek.

We parted ways once we found a long stretch of stream with solitude. He went upstream, out of sight, to let me get reacquainted with my long pole companion. I began to flick around a size 12 White Miller, more for rhythm and motion than for serious fishing. A nymph drifted along the bottom would have been a better choice, but I was happy to just be fly-fishing.

Several casts later, as my attention began to wander over some words in my mind, I heard an audible rise and felt a hard pull that brought me back to the water. A fish had hit the fly! I lifted my rod tip and felt the satisfying weight of a fish right as a trout surfaced and tail-flipped above the creek. My old technique came back as quickly as a boy does to his bike each spring. I stripped in the line, landed the fish, gently unhooked the fly from his jaw, and released him—or, he released me, rather—with a flash of a splash.

I was very surprised and happy, beaming with private pride that I had fooled a frisky rainbow trout. I leaned my rod against a tree and sat beside it on a wide, smooth stone. I took out the pen and small reporter's notebook from my front shirt pocket, flipped to a clean page, and began writing in an automatic way, writing words that were already written in my mind, words with a musical rhythm and structure unlike any words I had ever written before—

Sit beside the stream,
Write about your life . . . .

Appendix

Schuylkill & Wissahickon Fishes Caught On The Fly

*** Family CENTRARCHIDAE ***
1. Rock Bass —*Ambloplites rupestris*
2. Redbreast Sunfish —*Lepomis auritus*
3. Green Sunfish —*Lepomis cyanellus*
4. Pumpkinseed Sunfish —*Lepomis gibbosus*
5. Bluegill —*Lepomis macrochirus*
6. Longear Sunfish —*Lepomis megalotis*
7. Smallmouth Bass —*Micropterus dolomieu*
8. Largemouth Bass —*Micropterus salmoides*
9. Black Crappie —*Pomoxis nigromaculatus*

*** Family CLUPEIDAE ***
1. American Shad —*Alosa sapidissima*

*** Family ICTALURIDAE ***
1. Channel Catfish —*Ictalurus punctatus*

*** Family PERCICHTHYIDAE (or MORONIDAE) ***
1. White Perch —*Morone americana*
2. Striped Bass —*Morone saxatilis*

*** Family PERCHIDAE ***
1. Yellow Perch —*Perca flavescens*

*** Family SALMONIDAE ***
1. Rainbow Trout —*Oncorhynchus mykiss*
2. Brown Trout —*Salmo trutta*

Sources

Books

Gordon, Bernard Ludwig. *The Secret Lives Of Fishes*. Boston, MA. The Book & Tackle Shop. 1980.

Ingram, Jr., George H., Robert F. Marler, Robert R. Smith. *Fishing The Delaware Valley*. Philadelphia, PA. Temple University Press. 1997.

Landis, Dwight. *Trout Streams of Pennsylvania: An Angler's Guide*. 3rd Edition. Bellefonte, PA. Hempstead-Lyndell. 2000.

McClane, A. J. *The Encyclopedia Of Fish Cookery*. New York, NY. Holt, Reinhart and Winston. 1989.

Nemes, Sylvester. *The Soft-Hackled Fly*. Old Greenwich, CT. The Chatham Press. 1975.

Robbins, Chandler S., Bertel Bruun, Herbert S. Zim, and Arthur Singer. *Birds Of North America*. New York, NY. Golden Press. 1966.

Toll, Jean Barth, and Mildred S. Gillam. *Invisible Philadelphia*. Atwater Kent Museum. Philadelphia, PA. 1995.

Trench, Charles Pocklington Chenevix. *A History Of Angling*. Hart-Davis MacGibbon. London and Chicago. 1974.

Walton, Izaak. *The Compleat Angler*. New York, NY. Collier Books. 1962.

Woods, Craig. *The River As Looking Glass*. New York, NY. The Stephen Greene Press. Pelham Books. 1988.

Articles

Miko, David A. "Wissahickon Creek Questions." *Pennsylvania Angler & Boater*. March-April 1999.

Poe, Edgar Allan. "Morning On The Wissahiccon." *The Opal*. 1844.

Talleur, Dick. "Advanced Hornbergery." *American Angler*. March-April 2001.

Websites

◆ Bluebell Hill
  http://www.bluebellhill.org/default.htm
An online museum dedicated to the history and community of Bluebell Hill, which includes much of Fairmount Park and Wissahickon Creek.

◆ Friends of the Wissahickon
  http://www.fow.org/
A group dedicated to the preservation and promotion of the Wissahickon Valley.

◆ Pennsylvania Fish & Boat Commission
  http://sites.state.pa.us/Fish/mpag1.htm
The most complete online resource for information on the waterways and fisheries of the Commonwealth of Pennsylvania.

◆Pennsylvania Fly-Fishing
  http://www.paflyfish.com/
A website dedicated to the fly-fisher in Pennsylvania. Includes stocking and stream reports and a message board.

◆River Smallies
  http://www.riversmallies.com/index.html
An online meeting place for smallmouth bass anglers and their fish of choice. Includes how-to articles and message boards.

About The Author

ron P. swegman hooked his first brook trout on a Royal Coachman along the headwaters of the Pemigewasset River in New Hampshire. He was born and raised in Pittsburgh and educated at Penn State and the Poynter Institute for Media Studies. The author of a collection of poetry, *museum of buildings: poems*, he now lives in Center City Philadelphia, a metropolis made for angling, bicycling, and writing.
www.ronpswegman.com

Small-Stream Fly-Fishing
Jeff Morgan

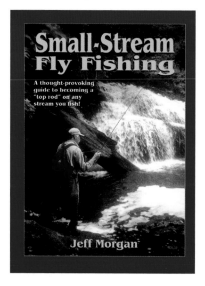

There are many myths surrounding small streams—they only hold small fish, they're for beginners and kids, they aren't a challenge, don't allow for versatility in techniques, and so on—in this book, Morgan addresses these myths and shares the realities of small-stream fishing. Topics covered include: the myths; best small-stream equipment; ecology; entomology and fly patterns; small-stream types; fly-fishing techniques; casting; reading the water; and more. If you're up for the challenge, maybe it's time to explore this fun and unique facet of fly-fishing. 8 1/2 x 11 inches, 128 pages.

SB: $24.95
ISBN: 1-57188-346-0
UPC: 0-81127-00180-4

Trout Stream Fly-Fishing
Harry Murray

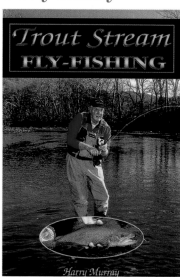

The purpose of this handy little guide is to enable you to refine your angling skills so you can enjoy fishing for trout on streams anywhere in the country. Murray has decades of experience fishing small streams, and shares important information such as: trout foods and fly selection; reading water; spotting trout; techniques for all seasons; mastering all water conditions; trout behavior and habitat; fly tackle; fly casting; hatches; fly plates; and more. 4 x 5 inches, 102 pages.

SB: $9.95   ISBN: 1-57188-281-2
UPC: 0-81127-00100-2

Ask for these books at your local fly/tackle shop or call toll-free to order:
1-800-541-9498 (8 to 5 p.s.t.) • www.amatobooks.com
Frank Amato Publications, Inc. • P.O. Box 82112 • Portland, Oregon 97282

Deer-Hair Fly-Tying Guidebook
Jack Pangburn

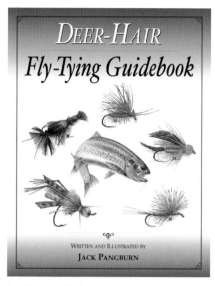

There are many ways to catch a fish, but catching one on a fly you've tied yourself is by far the most exciting and rewarding. Most food items trout feed on are of natural earth-tone colors, and there is no better way to imitate nature than to use what nature has to offer. Deer hair is one of the most versatile and popular natural materials used in fly tying, and in this book Jack Pangburn shows you how to combine deer hair and other elements to create a finished, fishable fly. Topics include: fly-tying materials • hooks • stacking • wrapping • dubbing • wings • flared bucktail • spinning • bundled bodies • 84 fly patterns, many with step-by-step tying instructions • and more. The beautiful, detailed illustrations give this book the feel of a personal streamside journal, add the crisp photography and informative text and this book gives you all the information you need to become a great tier of deer-hair flies. 8 1/2 x 1 inches, 64 pages.

SB: $14.95	ISBN: 1-57188-329-0	UPC: 0-81127-00162-0
Limited HB: $40.00	ISBN: 1-57188-330-4	UPC: 0-81127-00163-7

Northeast Trout, Salmon, and Steelhead Streams
John Mordock

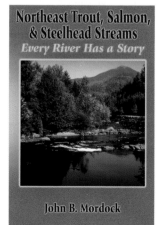

John Mordock has fished these rivers for decades, including such fabled waters as the Ausable, Battenkill, Housatonic, Willowemoc, Neversink, small Catskill trout streams, the Delaware, Esopus, Moosehead Lake rivers, the Salmon River in New York, and so many more. So much interesting and useful information is shared for each water covered, including its history, local characters, species and hatches, even accommodations and other attractions for the non-fishers traveling with you; all of this information and more is passed on in an entertaining way. 6 x 9 inches, 80 pages.

SB: $15.95   ISBN: 1-57188-311-8
UPC: 0-81127-00145-3

Fly Tying Made Clear and Simple
Skip Morris

With over 220 color photographs, expert tier show all the techniques you need to know. 73 different materials and 27 tools. Clear, precise advice tells you how to do it step-by-step. Dries, wets, streamers, nymphs, etc., included so that you can tie virtually any pattern. 8 1/2 x 11 inches, 80 pages.

SPIRAL SB: $19.95   ISBN: 1-878175-13-0
UPC: 0-66066-00103-0

SOFTBOUND: $19.95   ISBN: 1-57188-231-6
UPC: 0-81127-00131-6

DVD: $26.95   ISBN: 1-57188-365-7
UPC: 0-81127-00199-6

Great Smoky Mountains National Park Angler's Companion

Ian Rutter

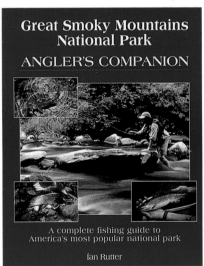

Ian Rutter unlocks the secrets of this gorgeous region, including: trout streams, game fish, fishing methods, fishing seasons, catching larger trout, trout flies, and more. Some of the streams are closed to fishing for the study and preservation of brook trout populations, but those that are open to fishing are described individually, including fish species, productive flies and techniques, stream features, access, easy-to-read icons, and more. If you are fortunate enough to fish this beautiful, historical area of America, this handbook will be your perfect guide. 8 1/2 x 11 inches, 64 pages.

SB: $16.95   ISBN: 1-57188-241-3
UPC: 0-66066-00495-6

Ask for these books at your local fly/tackle shop or call toll-free to order:
1-800-541-9498 (8 to 5 p.s.t.) • www.amatobooks.com
Frank Amato Publications, Inc. • P.O. Box 82112 • Portland, Oregon 97282

Nymph Fishing
Dave Hughes

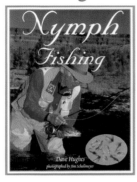

This masterful all-color, large-format book by one of America's favorite angling writers will teach you what you need to know to fish nymphs effectively, with crisp text and dramatic color photos by Jim Schollmeyer. Color plates and dressings of author's favorite nymphs. All the techniques and methods learned here will guarantee that on the stream or lake your nymph imitation will be fishing right! 8 1/2 x 11 inches, 56 pages.

SB: $19.95   ISBN: 1-57188-002-X
UPC: 0-66066-00192-4

Dry Fly Fishing
Dave Hughes

This beautifully written, all-color guide, will help make you a very competent dry-fly angler with chapters on: tackle, dry-fly selection, dry-fly casting techniques, fishing dry-flies on moving water and on lakes and ponds, hatches and matching patterns, and 60 of the best dries in color and with fly dressings. The information contained and attractive color presentation will really help you! 8 1/2 x 11 inches, 56 pages.

SB: $15.95   ISBN: 1-878175-68-8
UPC: 0-66066-00153-5

Hatch Guide For New England Streams
Thomas Ames, Jr.

New England's streams, and the insects and fish that inhabit them, have their own unique qualities that support an amazing diversity of insect species from all of the major orders. This book covers: reading water; presentations for New England streams; tackle; night fishing; and more. Ames discusses the natural and its behaviors and the three best flies to imitate it, including proper size and effective techniques. Tom's color photography of the naturals and their imitations is superb! Full color. 4 x 4 inches, 272 pages; insect and fly plates.

SB: $19.95   ISBN: 1-57188-210-3
UPC: 0-66066-00424-6

Fit to Fish: How to Tackle Angling Injuries
Stephen L. Hisey, PT and Keith R. Berend, MD

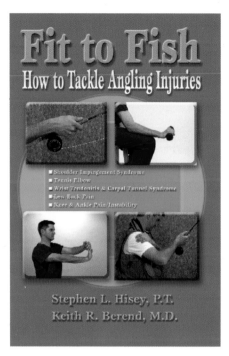

Survey all your fishing buddies and you'll find that the vast majority of them suffer from some kind of shoulder, elbow, or wrist pain due to casting all day long. Fit to Fish shares common disorders prevalent in fly anglers, explains the causes, and describes treatment and prevention techniques utilizing conditioning, stretching, and exercise, and also includes many photographs that greatly enhance this text. Berend, a surgeon, and Hisey, a physical therapist, have 75 years of combined experience treating the human body. Topics covered include: Pain and its origins; self treatment; shoulder impingement syndrome; tendonitis and Carpal Tunnel; low back pain; knee and ankle pain and instability; glossary; and more. 6 x 9 inches, 130 pages.

SB: $19.95   ISBN: 1-57188-354-1
UPC: 0-81127-00188-0

Subscribe to Flyfishing & Tying Journal

We're confident you'll love *FTJ*. Each information-filled, 88 page, full-color issue will make your time on the water more successful, your time at the tying bench more enjoyable. Within our pages you'll find North America's most helpful fly-fishing authors.

So go ahead, expect the best. *Flyfishing & Tying Journal* is your magazine.

For more information on starting your FTS subscription,
Call 800.541.9498
or go to our website at: www.amatobooks.com